Speculative Bubbles and Monetary Policy

Speculative Bubbles and Monetary Policy

A Theory Based on Japanese Experience

Masayuki Otaki

LEXINGTON BOOKS
Lanham • Boulder • New York • London

Published by Lexington Books
An imprint of The Rowman & Littlefield Publishing Group, Inc.
4501 Forbes Boulevard, Suite 200, Lanham, Maryland 20706
www.rowman.com

6 Tinworth Street, London, United Kingdom, SE11 5AL

British Library Cataloguing in Publication Information Available

Library of Congress Cataloging-in-Publication Data Available

ISBN: 978-1-4785-4914-1 (cloth : alk. paper)
ISBN: 978-1-4785-4915-8 (electronic)

∞™ The paper used in this publication meets the minimum requirements of American National Standard for Information Sciences—Permanence of Paper for Printed Library Materials, ANSI/NISO Z39.48-1992.

Printed in the United States of America

Contents

List of Figures

Acknowledgments

To complete this book, I owe much thanks to the liberal atmosphere of the Research Institute of Capital Formation at the Development Bank of Japan (RICF). Keynes writes in *The General Theory*, "The writer of a book such as this, treading along unfamiliar paths, is extremely dependent on criticism and conversation if he is to avoid an undue proportion of mistakes."

Needless to say, it is impolite to compare this small book with *The General Theory*. However, I feel acutely encouraged by liberal discussions at RICF, especially with Morio Kuninori, Hiroaki Jindo, and Susumu Cato that advanced my writing immensely. I am also grateful to the management foresight of Mitsuhiro Usui, Masaaki Komiya, and Hideo Oishi for maintaining a pragmatic environment at RICF, which is uncommon in Japan.

Special thanks must be devoted to Shozo Miyamoto, who kindly provided many comments about Part I, and to Takuya Kuroda, who gave me opportunities for progressing my theoretical research.

In addition, this book is supported by JSPS KAKENHI Grant Numbers JP23530215, JP26380232, and JP17K03618.

Finally, to my generous and thoughtful wife Midori, who fully supported my writing of this book even when I was hindered by illness.

Masayuki Otaki
March 15, 2018

Introduction

This book provides a group of macroeconomic theories, which are mutually consistent and cohesive, for understanding the economic history of the Japanese economy. Japan once fascinated many other economies with its excellent economic performance from the late 1950s to the early 1980s. However, after the burst of the bubble boom, and especially after the Asian financial crisis in 1997, the economy was decelerated and hampered by pathological public debt accumulation. If this political and economic situation persists, it will be a tremendous burden on future generations.

The radical quantitative easing policy (QE policy), which aims to accelerate inflation, is crucially related to this phenomenon. However, against the intent of monetary authorities, the economy experienced prominent disinflation and/or mild deflation around the turn of the twenty-first century. Ironically, other advanced economies began to refocus on Japan in this respect. The aim of this book is to elucidate the acute economic causes of this seemingly paradoxical phenomenon.

This book is composed of two parts. Part I describes the economic history of the Japanese economy from the 1980s to 2010s concisely and is based on theories extended in Part II. The following three points are emphasized: First, an analysis of why speculative bubbles in land and stock were exponentially expanded in the late 1980s; second, how the Japanese economy prospered until the Asian financial crisis in 1997 and how the economy experienced ambiguities and uncertainties due to large amounts of non-performing debt as a result of the bursting of the speculative bubbles; third, how the structural reform, which decisively relied on neoliberal thought, decomposed the Japanese firm from an organic entity into a simple assembly of production resources. Consequently, the efficiency of the economy was aggravated through the depletion of information processing skills that was the most advantageous feature of Japanese firms in the 1980s. In addition, the efficiency of the economy was negatively impacted by the radical QE policy, which is the other side of the same coin of incompetence in fiscal discipline.

Part II includes theories that support the historical narrative in Part I. Chapter 2 deals with the fundamental theory of this book and advocates an endogenous price stickiness that is peculiar to a monetary economy. Chapter 3 is devoted to elucidating how speculative bubbles are generated and exhibits how the consequence of burst bubbles burdens subsequent generations. In contrast to extant research on speculative bubbles, my theory succeeds in showing how the rate of return for bubbly assets can exceed the market interest rate. Chapter 4 analyzes the relationships among labor productivity stagnation, the radical QE policy, and disinflation. Labor productivity stagnation, *ceteris paribus*, brings a shortage of supply capacity relative to aggregate demand. Accordingly, the current price level becomes high compared to the future price level, and when the market adjusts to such an exogenous shock, disinflation progresses. The radical QE policy forces an economy to provide additional savings. To promote savings, it is inevitable that the rate of return for money increases. This implies that the radical QE policy is one of the most important causes of disinflation. Chapter 5 considers the equilibrium selection problem in a monetary economy. Owing to indeterminacy of the equilibrium, which is peculiar to a monetary economy, the economy brings about not only a Keynesian solution but also the quantity theoretic solution. Using Ramsey's probability theory, I assert that a Keynesian equilibrium is more likely to emerge than the equilibrium supported by the quantity theoretic rational expectations.

In the following, I introduce the contents in more detail.

ABOUT PART I

First, the description of Japanese economic history is extended to the 1980s compared with Otaki (2015b). This extension is purposeful. The economic structure of Japan that prevailed before the Asian financial crisis in 1997 was entirely different from that in the present. To underline the seriousness of the structural reform enforced by the Koizumi administration at the beginning of the twenty-first century, it is vital to understand the socioeconomic institution in the heyday of the Japanese economy.

Numerous books and papers in economics and management science deal with how the Japanese economy achieved prosperity during the 1980s, although most of them have been forgotten. One of the most serious reasons why the content of these writings has become almost saturated and/or out of date is not only that the authors' observation is superfluous but also that the provided assertions are not analytical.

By contrast, this book focuses on the fundamental economic institution that sustained the prosperity, namely, the *internalization of the positive economic externality among employees*. In general, the pragmatic information exchanged between employees and the corresponding precise interpretation in line with the context is crucial for heightening efficiency in a firm. This undeniable fact implies that a significant but intangible positive externality exists between employees because of the inseparability of jobs, and how to internalize such an externality is vital for business excellence. I show in Part I that the prominence of Japanese employment practices (a kind of autonomous order) enhanced such internalization. Corresponding mathematical models are shown by Fukao and Otaki (1993) and Horiuchi and Otaki (2017).

Second, I emphasize that the seed of the disaster of explosive speculative bubbles and busts already existed when Japan was enjoying prosperity during the mid-1980s. Abundant liquidity derived from huge current account surpluses prompted Japanese firms to earn from financial investment rather than capital investment. This tendency was accelerated by the rapid appreciation of the Japanese yen due to the Plaza Agreement because the price elasticity of Japanese manufacturing goods was not high and such rapid appreciation triggered a massive inflow of US dollars. Thus, in conjunction with a historically low interest policy of the Bank of Japan, such prosperity, which heavily depended on exports, laid the platform for the bubble.

Third, I clarify that the industrial policy toward financial intermediaries, namely the so-called "the guarded convoy procedure," amplified the bubble. Theoretically, this conventional policy may have provoked morally hazardous behavior under limited liability. This discussion is closely connected to that in chapter 3. That is, such policy implied that the monetary authority benevolently pledged to rescue any financial intermediary that fell into a management crisis to the extent that the intermediary was acting in good faith and behaving according to the guidelines of the authority. This convention slackened discipline about downside risks, and hence financial intermediaries leapt to easy-going speculation as soon as prominent high-return assets emerged.

Fourth, I point out the significant rift in Japanese economic history around the Asian financial crisis in 1997. Many Japanese economists dub the 1990s "the lost decade" in the sense that the Japanese did not possess sufficient vigor to reform their devastating economic situation. However, this assertion is improper and/or imprecise. Although the non-performing debt problem resulting from the bursting of the bubble was a serious economic issue, it was regarded as solvable. Indeed, even as the growth rate decelerated, people unrelated to financial, immobile assets and construction industries still enjoyed the warm glow of prosperity. Many books boast about the excellence of Japanese firms even in the first half of the 1990s.

As Allen (1931) describes with regard to the land and stock market boom of the US economy in the 1920s, substantial time lapses until people find they have fallen into a devastating economic situation. The domestic financial panic contaminated by the Asian financial crisis in 1997 brought home reality to the Japanese. This is my historical view.

Applying this view to the post-Asian financial crisis era helps explain why the structural reform enforced by the Koizumi administration from the turn of the century aimed to nullify the existing Japanese socioeconomic institution that sustained prosperity and instead to conduct rapid and incessant deregulation based on neoliberal thought. Judging from the current appalling economic consequences, such a nexus of policies was short-sighted and too aggressive. In other words, the market failure in the late 1980s was replaced by the failure of government in the twenty-first century.

Finally, I elucidate the pathology from which the current Japanese economy suffers: prominent and persistent disinflation juxtaposed by stagnation in labor productivity and radical quantitative easing (QE). This assertion is formally proven by using a mathematical model, as shown in chapter 4.

Every existing theory predicts that these economic factors necessarily accelerate inflation. This is partly because these theories genuinely assume the quantity theory of money and partly because the models adopted are static. According to the quantity theory of money, which asserts that, sooner or later, price hikes occur proportionately to nominal money supply, radical QE should eventually induce inflation. Meanwhile, stagnation in labor productivity causes a leftward shift of the aggregate supply curve, and hence inflation occurs in this case, too. This logic is a simple application of the traditional supply-shock model proposed by Bruno and Sachs (1985). Thus, the current economic situation is an anomaly from the point of view of traditional theory.

However, if we extend the theory to a dynamic and monetary economy in the same way as Lucas (1972), against his assertion, we find that an important tautology peculiar to monetary economy holds. That is, *the value of money (the inverse of price level) is determined by rational expectations concerning the future value of money itself.* Whenever people believe in the preciousness of money in the future, they appreciate its current value, and vice versa. This assertion implies that the equilibrium price level sequence, *ceteris paribus*, can be unaffected by a change in nominal money supply to the extent that people's confidence in the value of money is not disrupted. In this sense, money is intrinsically non-neutral to the real economy.

In such a context, disinflation along with radical QE can be explained as follows. Assume that the current price level is kept invariant by an increase in nominal supply. Then, savings (i.e., demand for money) should be boosted to equilibrate the money market. Accordingly, the rate of return for money hoarding (the inverse of the inflation rate) rises. In other words, people become more pious about the future value of money and thus disinflation emerges.

Similarly, stagnation in labor productivity causes disinflation. Such stagnation, *ceteris paribus*, causes potential excess demand in the goods market. To the extent that people are confident in the current value of money (the inverse of the price level), the rate of return for money hoarding rises to make them postpone consumption. Therefore, stagnation in labor productivity is one of the most serious factors that causes disinflation.

ABOUT PART II

Part II is composed of a group of theories developed after the publication of Otaki (2015a). All the chapters in Part II are written to clarify the social cohesion with Part I. I write each chapter for undergraduate audiences. According to my experiences in my lectures, it would be desirable to reduce the number of equations by introducing some heuristic logic and geometric methods based on elementary microeconomic theory.

This procedure is especially crucial for the extension of the fundamental theory in chapter 2, because the rest of the chapters in Part II depend entirely on this theory. Such an intuitive explanation places much importance on economic logic rather than mathematical technique.

Chapter 3 presents an analytical tool for considering the economic consequences of the bubble and its bursting from the late 1980s to the 1990s. A bubble asset whose original expected rate of return is zero is introduced into the model in addition to money. The most remarkable feature of this chapter is the definition of speculative bubbles, which allows that the expected rate of return under limited liability for a bubble asset exceeds the nominal rate of interest. This definition could be regarded as innovative because most existing articles about speculative bubbles are obliged to assume, against reality, that the rate of return for a bubble asset is equal to that of a safety asset (see, for example, Blanchard and Watson 1982). This property of the model illustrates the irresponsible behavior of Japanese financial intermediaries during the bubble boom from the late 1980s to the beginning of the 1990s.

Meanwhile, this chapter emphasizes that the bubble ultimately provoked a grievance that non-performing debt, which was a consequence of the bust, was converted into public debt via radical fiscal/monetary policy. The current illicit accumulation of public debt in the Japanese economy stems from this conversion. In addition, this chapter proves that the redemption of such public debt places an additional burden on future generations.

This assertion implies that, in general, speculative bubbles are undesirable from the perspective of intergenerational ethics.

The model in chapter 4 aims to capture economic phenomena peculiar to advanced economies in the twenty-first century: the coexistence of labor-productivity stagnation, radical monetary policy, and disinflation. I emphasize that no other theory exists that can explain this worldwide anomaly of the market economy. An intuitive discussion on this chapter was already provided together with the historical review of the Japanese economy in the twenty-first century in Part I. This chapter focuses on the mathematical and rigorous structure of the theory in relation to the fundamental theory proposed in chapter 2. Here, I will also use intensive economic-theoretic logic rather than mathematics for undergraduate students.

In addition, there is another originality in this model. The theory predicts the aftermath of relentless QE: stagflation. Stagflation can be regarded as a collapse of speculative bubbles in money itself. Whenever people excessively believe in the intrinsic value of money despite QE, as discussed above, disinflation ensues. This phenomenon can be interpreted as a kind of speculative bubble in money. Accordingly, if every economic agent finds that excess liquidity is provided relative to potential production capacity and regards money as redundant, current price levels rise (i.e., the value of money depreciates). Equivalently, this reduces the purchasing power of money holders and the economy will slump. Thus, disbelief in the future value of money may coincide with inflation and stagnation (i.e., stagflation). In other words, acute suspicion about the value of money, urged by incessant and radical QE, results in the collapse of speculative bubbles in money.

Furthermore, the massive default of public debt is the other side of the same coin of stagflation in the sense that the total value of monetary assets devalues prominently. Unless substantial amounts of tax are additionally levied to redeem public debt and/or lessen nominal money stock, the consequence of radical QE will be awful.

Finally, chapter 5 analyzes a change in the belief in the rational confidence in money. Although equilibrium inflation is endogenously determined in my model, the absolute price level is undetermined, and thus some arbitrariness exists in the theory. However, such a property comes from the genetic structure of the monetary economy. That is, the aforementioned tautology, which asserts that the current value of money is determined by rational expectations concerning its future value, is upheld in a monetary economy.

Accordingly, there are infinite rational expectations equilibria in the model. I assume that money is an *absolute* substance in the sense that people believe in its intrinsic value and that such value is unaffected by a change in nominal money supply. However, there is an alternative economic school concerning the value of money: the quantity theory of money, which regards money as a *relative* substance. According to this theory, the purchasing power of money is invariant with the quantity of money, while an increase in nominal money supply only causes a proportionate hike in prices. In this chapter, I show that such a rational expectations equilibrium is also viable under my theory. Consequently, one can ascertain the depth of the theory extended in this book.

Moreover, by relying on Ramsey (1926), I examine which of the two ways of thinking is the more plausible equilibrium. While the quantity theory presumes that people possess precise information on the structure of the economy as Lucas (1972) shows, money can become an absolute substance only by believing in its intrinsic value. As such, the latter rational belief requires less elaboration. According to Ramsey's probability theory, less elaboration creates higher confidence. In this sense, the quantity theory of money is less persuasive than the Keynesian-type rational expectations equilibrium, which I use throughout the book. This assertion is not refuted by reality.

REFERENCES

Allen, Franklin L., *Only Yesterday: An Informal History of the 1920s*, New York: Harper & Row, Publishers, 1931.

Blanchard, Oliver J., and Mark W. Watson, "Bubbles, Rational Expectations, and Financial Markets," *NBER Working Paper*, No. w945 (July 1982).

Bruno, Michael and Jeffery D. Sachs, *Economics of Worldwide Stagflation*, Cambridge, MA: Harvard University Press, 1985.

Fukao, Kyoji and Masayuki Otaki, "Accumulation of Human Capital and the Business Cycle," *Journal of Political Economy* 101 no. 1 (February 1993), 73–99.

Horiuchi, Kozo and Masayuki Otaki, *Doctor Osamu Shimomura's Legacy and the Post War Japanese Economy*, Singapore: Springer, 2017.

Lucas, Robert. E. Jr., "Expectations and the Neutrality of Money," *Journal of Economic Theory* 4 (1972): 103–24.

Otaki, Masayuki. *Keynesian Economics and Price Theory: Re-orientation of a Theory of Monetary Economy*, Tokyo: Springer, 2015a.

———. *The Origin of the Prolonged Stagnation in Contemporary Japanese Economy: Factitious Deflation and the Meltdown of the Japanese Firm as an Entity*, Singapore: Routledge, 2015b.

Ramsey, Frank. P., "Truth and Probability," (1926), in *Philosophical Papers*, edited by D. H. Mellor, Cambridge: Cambridge University Press, 1990.

Part I

HISTORICAL NARRATIVE

Chapter 1

A Concise Economic History of Japan

Prosperity and Crisis

ABSTRACT

This chapter deals with the economic history of the Japanese economy from the 1980s to the first half of the 2010s. The 1980s was the most robust and prosperous period for Japan after World War II. Efficient information processing skills, which originated from and were cultivated during the high growth era (from the late 1950s to 1972), played a crucial role. This finding implies that Japan's prosperity was supported by Japanese employment practices, which provided a kind of insurance against the risk of intensive sunk-cost investment in human capital, as well as good business opportunities in the US. Nevertheless, the affluent liquidity provided by (a) the Bank of Japan (BOJ), which was the unanticipated byproduct of a low interest policy against the rapid appreciation of the Japanese yen brought about by the Plaza Agreement, and (b) significant earnings derived from overseas markets triggered the bubble boom in the stock and immobile asset market.

The current economic crisis of the Japanese economy began in the 1990s. The bubble burst in early 1991, leaving a huge amount of non-performing debt. However, Japan still enjoyed shaky prosperity until the Asian financial crisis of 1997–1998, and the event of this time revealed the fragility of the Japanese economy. In this sense, the assertion that the 1990s was "the lost decade" is not a truism but rather clumsy enthusiasm. Such ephemeral prosperity was sustained by expansionary fiscal policy and a compromise rescue policy for financial intermediaries, which is the real reason for current excess public debt.

Around the turn of the century, most Japanese changed their minds about the employment system. They considered that Japanese employment practices, which were autonomous devices to encourage sunk-cost investment in human capital, had become out of date, and that deregulation in the labor and capital markets had become unavoidable in order to regain the robustness of the Japanese economy. Thereafter, the structural reform advanced by the Koizumi cabinet decided the fate of Japan. Although the administration changed from the Liberal Democratic Party to the Democratic Party for a short while, policymakers' way of thinking remained anchored in neoliberal economic thought. The most notable characteristic is that Japan's advantage in voluntary and efficient information processing has been disrupted.

Finally, this chapter analyzes so-called Abenomics, which comprises aggressive fiscal-monetary policy and enhancement of libertarian corporate governance. This discussion elucidates why Keynesians compromise or submit to neoliberal thought.

1.1 INTRODUCTION

This chapter presents a concise history of the Japanese economy, which centers on the financial sector from the 1980s to the present. I spent this time as an undergraduate student, graduate school student, and university teacher. In this sense, this concise history is a living testimony.

The 1980s was the heyday of the Japanese economy. The manufacturing sector produced high-quality, robust, and compact goods symbolized by SONY's *Walkman.* These products swept the global market. Although it might seem difficult to believe, Ezra Vogel's *Japan as Number 1* was a best-seller and most teachers in economics and business claimed that the economic power of Japan exceeded that of the US. This evidence reflects how prosperous the Japanese economy was. The Plaza Agreement of 1985 caused the appreciation of the exchange rate by 120 Japanese yen (JPY) against the US dollar (USD). However, the recession was not as serious as expected because of the historically low interest policy of the BOJ.

Soon after, the bubble era arrived, during which many Japanese became caught up in land and stock speculation. In other words, around 1988, Japan was thrust into the so-called bubble boom. However, when assets became expensive and ordinary people were unable to purchase them, the bubble burst. The reason for the bubble bursting is *fundamental values*, which are the upper-bound prices. The value of land originates from the fact that land is ultimately used for housing and building, not only for hoarding. Stock value is sustained by the size of dividends obtained through purchasing. The fundamental value comprises such principles. Accordingly, whenever market prices exceed this value, individuals find there is no gain from purchasing such assets, and thus, the bubble bursts.

It is not easy to identify the precise time that the bubble burst, but most researchers estimate the collapse began in 1990. To summarize, the Plaza Agreement (1985) and the bursting of the bubble (1991) were turning points for the Japanese economy.

It is not an over-exaggeration to state that the Japanese economy of the 1990s was focused on dealing with the effects of the burst bubble. Public debts increased by 400 trillion JPY during this decade. Even though public debt was put into this use, there is no doubt that a huge amount of money was consumed by the depreciation of non-performing debt, which was an implicit subsidy for financial intermediaries and by public investment to rescue the construction and real estate industry, which faced serious management crises. Historically, the fiscal deficit at that time paralyzed fiscal discipline and resulted in the pathological accumulation of public debt, an outcome of which most conscientious Japanese are afraid.

Nevertheless, I dare say that for those who were not affected by the bubble boom, the 1990s was not a difficult time because the expansion of public investment sustained the economy until the Asian financial crisis in 1997 revealed how deep the calamity was. In general, speculative bubbles maintain the economy not only when they are expanding, but also when they are collapsing, because public funds are available to offset the huge losses. In fact, the average growth rate of GDP was around two percent annually throughout the 1990s.[1]

One might consider that two percent annual growth would not enrich Japan that much. However, this assumption would be incorrect. It is important to distinguish between growth rate and actual number. For example, while Japanese GDP in 1990 was JPY 451 trillion (about USD 4 trillion), it was JPY 513 trillion (about USD 6 trillion) in 1997, which was the same level as 2007. In addition, it should be noted that Japanese GDP increased by JPY 35 trillion in the year from 1989 to 1990. In summary, the Japanese economy before the Asian financial crisis was enjoying the legacy of the bubble boom.[2] It was not "the lost decade," a term superficially created by some economists for the 1990s.

This is a typical ex-post regression. Almost no Japanese considered that the burst of the bubble impaired the economy so deeply. During the period from 1980 to 1985, the Japanese economy was sound and growing steadily, and GDP amounted to JPY 330 trillion in 1985. Thus, the latter half of the 1990s expanded Japan's GDP by JPY 120 trillion. It would not have been unnatural for the Japanese to be blind to greed owing to such rapid growth. Consequently, until the abrupt occurrence of the Asian financial crisis, Japan enjoyed economic prosperity although the Japanese were vaguely anxious.

The Asian financial crisis, which originated in Thailand, was triggered in 1997. This calamity aggravated the Japanese economy quite significantly.

Not only were exports to East Asia curtailed, but also fatigued major financial intermediaries went bankrupt, among them the Yamaichi Securities, the Long-Term Credit Bank of Japan (Nihon Choki Shinyo Ginko), Nippon Credit Bank (Nippon Saiken Shinyo Ginko), and Hokkaido Takushoku Bank. This was a kind of financial panic and signaled the downturn of long-run expectations of Japanese companies. Capital investment in Japan was JPY 140 trillion, which decreased by about JPY 10 trillion during the Asian financial crisis, and thereafter to around JPY 100 trillion. This factor is one of the serious causes of the prolonged stagnation of the Japanese economy from around the turn of the century.

The Koizumi administration advanced deregulation and liberalization policies to tackle the economic crisis. This nexus of policies was dubbed "the structural reform" (Kozo Kaikaku). The philosophy of the structural reform has become the foundation for subsequent economic policies despite cabinet changes. The background of the philosophy is as follows. In the prosperous 1980s, the Japanese manufacturing industry was based on the excellent social cohesion of society or companies, a rare phenomenon in the US. The structural reform conversely regarded such cohesion as an obstacle to free competition and weakened the incentive to compete. Therefore, its natural consequence was deregulation and liberalization, which possibly annihilated intrinsic cohesion.

Deregulation in the labor market is one of the most notable policies of the structural reform. According to the Labor Force Survey (The Ministry of Internal Affairs and Communications), regular workers comprised about ninety percent of all employees in 2003, but this ratio decreased to sixty percent in 2013. This implies *de facto* fortification of the right to fire because it is difficult to fire regular workers but not non-regular workers. This deregulation of the labor market turned the concept of lifetime employment upside down by emphasizing that the cohesion of society and/or firms is vital for economic prosperity. This was a mainstream concept during the 1980s and 1990s.

In other words, structural reform regards the very existence of the cohesion of organizations and society as a source for the origin of wasteful rents for idle people. Since young Japanese have grown up with and learned such a tendency, it is difficult for them to understand the Japanese way of life before the bubble boom.

Labor market deregulation has brought a surge in foreign direct investment (FDI) aimed at utilizing the cheap labor force in East Asian economies. In other words, most Japanese manufacturing industries considered that high wages, which enriched the standard of Japanese workers, should be substituted by a cheap and abundant East Asian labor force and that such structural change would heighten the Japanese economy's competitiveness. It was necessary to achieve this labor force substitution to close domestic branches and factories. Accordingly, labor market deregulation, which strengthens the right to fire workers, was a convenient vehicle. As precisely discussed below, the surge of FDI had severe consequences. The unemployment rate of unskilled young generations soared and wages, especially those of blue-collar workers, decreased rapidly and turbulently. In addition, FDI is one of the major causes of stagnant domestic capital investment as stated earlier in the introduction.

Furthermore, there is another serious pitfall associated with the surge of FDI. It should be noted that the key currency is (was) that of the US (UK). The key currency country is almost free from exchange rate risk, because most international economic transactions are enforced by these currencies. Since the JPY is not the key currency, the value of earned overseas profits in JPY possibly varies with volatile exchange rates.

For example, when an overseas affiliate considers remitting its USD earnings to headquarters in Japan, the affiliate must sell USD earnings in exchange for JPY. It should be noted that huge numbers of overseas affiliates and branch offices exist today. Accordingly, when they sell the USD at the same time in the foreign exchange market, the exchange rate appreciates drastically. Thus, the affiliates' earnings in JPY depreciate and the remitters lose substantial amounts of money. Consequently, we find that it is not easy for a home country to benefit from FDI. Under a flexible exchange rate system with a key currency, an increase in the domestic unemployment rate, reduction of wages, and high profit retention in overseas affiliates are unavoidable consequences as the current Japanese experience shows.[3]

Besides the surge of FDI, which was triggered by structural reform, the Japanese economy faces another serious problem: an aging society and population reduction. This problem not only curtails potential production capacity, but also provokes fiscal crisis. At the start of the 2000s, the burst bubble had settled, and public investment decreased from an annual average of JPY 28 trillion (in the 1990s) to JPY 19 trillion (in the 2000s). Nonetheless, the stock of public debt soared from JPY 733 trillion to JPY 1065 trillion (National Account: Cabinet Office), which implies that public debt increased by 33 JPY trillion on average. What caused such a tremendous deficit?

A table in the National Accounts of Japan "Precise Table on Transfer from the General Government to Household (Social Security)" (*Ippan Seifu kara Kakei eno Iten Meisaihyo* [*Shakai Hosho Kankei*]) records, item by item, how much money is transferred from the government to households as social security expenditure. Such transfers involve, for example, public pensions, public health insurance, the Latter-Stage Elderly Healthcare System (Kouki Koreisha Iryo), and the Nursing-Care Insurance (Kaigo Hoken). These data are based on the concept that the government collects taxes on behalf of the beneficiaries from taxpayers, and transfers the collected taxes to beneficiaries. In other words, the government is regarded as the intermediary of the social security service. It should be noted that the total sum of the social security provided exceeds the government revenue from the taxes and/or fees, which implies that the excess expenditure is financed by the issuance of public debt. Social security expenditure amounted to JPY 108 trillion in 2012, an increase of JPY 30 trillion from 2000. There is no denying that such a rapid increase in social security expenditure consists of a non-negligible part of the huge amount of public debt accumulation.

The beneficiaries of social security expenditure are mainly senior people. The National Institution of Population and Social Security Research predicts that Japan's population will fall by 40 million over the next 30 years. Consequently, a smaller number of taxpayers will be forced to sustain a far larger number of beneficiaries of social security. This projection implies that public debt accumulation will accelerate. I do not assert that the government should redeem the entire accumulated debt, which amounts to JPY 1,400 trillion. Nevertheless, it must be noted acutely that nominal assets are generally confident as long as they are exchangeable for goods at any time desired. Accordingly, the Japanese economy must strive to reduce public debt to a level at which public debt holders become confident of their assets. Thus, levying more taxes is unavoidable in the short term. In addition, the standard of Japanese social security must be reconsidered.

1.2 THE 1980s: FROM PROSPERITY TO FANATICISM

1.2.1 Japanese Employment Practice

In this subsection, I deal with the 1980s. Japan recorded GDP of JPY 240 trillion in 1980, which is less than half of the current GDP. Did many Japanese in those days regard themselves as poor with dismal futures? The answer is definitely no. Japan managed to overcome the second oil crisis in the latter half of the 1970s by undertaking energy-saving investment and heightening the efficiency of production processes, and thus, the Japanese economy achieved sound economic growth. In addition, it should be noted that the stock of public debt remained at JPY 126 trillion, which is only one-tenth that of 2016. In other words, Japan doubled its GDP in exchange for soaring public debt during the 4 decades since the 1980s. Put differently, while GDP grew only JPY 7 trillion per annum, public debt accumulated at a rate of JPY 30 trillion per annum. This is proof that the economy was far from achieving high efficiency.

Throughout this era, there were no IT utilities such as internet and smart phones.[4] As a result, was production efficiency significantly lower than the current era when no business can survive without IT facilities? The answer is also negative. Japanese corporations, which achieved excellent economic performance, were the focus of many researchers in this era. In particular, the Japanese labor market, whose characteristics were quite different from that of the US, was studied intensively. Japanese employment practice, which consisted of lifetime employment (Shushin Koyo Sei), seniority wage (Nenko Joretsu Chingin), and enterprise unions (Kigyobetsu Kumiai), was a most mysterious system attracting the curiosity of not only foreigners but also Japanese economists. Below, I explain the function of these systems, which emerged autonomously.

First, lifetime employment is a convention by which most Japanese work for one corporation until their retirement. Until the structural reform began, job conversion was an exceptional action. This contrasts with today's young Japanese who consider conversion a rite of passage. Although one strand of research advocates the view that lifetime employment is not limited to Japan, there is no denying that such a convention has been prominent in Japan, even within small companies, leading the employment environment to be far more stable than at present.

Then, why was such a convention sustained during the fifty years following World War II? Several schools tackled this subject. Late Professor Masahiko Aoki is one of the eminent researchers in this field,[5] which commonly asserted that it is a virtue that Japanese inherently possess the propensity for respecting cohesion despising selfishness. Economists and sociologists belonging to this school have claimed such a propensity nurtures coordination within firms, and as a result, Japanese firms have achieved high performance. These implicit and dense networks have been extended between the private and public sectors. This academic school emphasized these aspects as the acute origins of the Japanese economy's excellence. Let us call this the Aoki school.

Such an allegation was a rehash of the Marxian theory of state monopoly capitalism (Kokka Dokusen Shihon Shugi). It is not accidental that Professor Aoki had been a Marxist. The difference between the theory of state monopoly capitalism and the Aoki school centers on the protagonist of the economy. The Aoki school emphasizes the initiative of the private sector, which implies that the inherent Japanese coordination system benefits all Japanese while state monopoly capitalism enriches only people with strong relationships with the government. The Aoki school contains the following decisive drawback. If Japanese are cooperative while Anglo-Americans are not, then Anglo-Americans lack economic rationality. It seems to me that the thinking of the Aoki school contains chauvinism, provoked by the ephemeral prosperity of Japan. I consider it difficult for Japanese millennials to imagine that such thinking was common among advanced economies.

However, it should be noted that fashion dictates such matters. The other side of the same coin is the excessive belief in the US economy, a phenomenon that might be destroyed by US President Donald Trump. In general, the structure of an economy is prescribed by its climate, culture, and history, and hence, economic prosperity cannot be achieved only by mimicking or transplanting another economy's convention regardless of its own inherent characteristics.

In this sense, the embrace of Japan during the 1980s and excess Americanization, dubbed globalization, are the other sides of the same coin and do not have deep and logical roots. It should be noted that zealous thinking contains ephemeral and inessential factors in itself.

Why, then, did the lifetime employment convention autonomously emerge? Let us approach this problem from the point of view of economic rationality, not from the transcendent approach described above. The most important economic factor is the characteristic of skills nurtured within firms.

What was the nature of skills that were intensively nurtured in the Japanese firm until the 1980s? In general, graduates of natural sciences have visible skills, by which they can develop production processes and invent new goods. However, there are incomparably more numbers of graduates who have studied social sciences, humanities, and literature in Japan than those who have studied natural sciences. Although most of their skills are invisible, what is the nature of skills that are required and nurtured by them? If they consider that their jobs require no skills, and it is enough for them simply to follow a boss's order, then they will be sure to fail in their business lives. Since the average wage per annum of graduates with college diplomas amounts to JPY 6.8 million (for a forty-year-old male) according to the Wage Census 2015, and this wage was higher than that of graduates with high-school diplomas by JPY 1.3 million, college diplomas with no special skills will be substituted by high-school diplomas.

It must be noted that social sciences and humanities are sciences that reflect the natures of human beings and societies, and aim to contribute to welfare. In other words, those who studied social sciences and humanities are eagerly requested to nurture and furnish *information processing skills*. This is because such sciences are based on excellent inspection of human nature and can be applied to analyze specific characteristics of the constituents of organizations.

In addition, we must note that information processing skills contain skills for internalizing positive externalities that are brought by acquisition and/or production of information. Each employee has a different view of and information on team work jobs. Permeated skills are necessary for converging different views and constructing a consistent and productive business. Redundant information should be screened out. Information provided by employees cannot be vitalized until only meaningful pieces of information are extracted. An excellent senior officer should be in charge of such internalization.

Skills for developing a new market are a typical example of such internalization. Effective market research needs not only statistical analysis with numerical data, but also *organic* analysis on social networks and/or human relations. Even though numerical analysis suggests good business opportunities, whether or not the company can obtain new customers ultimately depends on its *reliability*, as perceived by potential customers. As Akerlof (1970) and Stiglitz and Weiss (1981) showed, there is serious informational asymmetry in the quality of goods between customers and companies. Customers do not possess as sufficient information as do companies that produce the goods.[6] Then with other things kept equal (which implies that the quality of competing goods is substantially identical), reliability matters.

Reliability comprises judgment about the company's sincerity with the occurrence of unexpected trouble, which is written either in or cannot be written in the contract, and the belief of customers in the company's reliability itself. Accordingly, to develop such reliability, investigation with warm hearts for customers is indispensable, and hence, knowledge of fundamental social sciences and humanities should be deployed.

Meanwhile, reliability belongs to a concept that holds only in the long run. In the short run, con artists can survive. However, in the long run, everything is revealed. This stringent fact implies that patience is also a constituent of reliability. Thus, it takes a long time to nurture information processing skills, which are based on studies in college and extended through learning by doing at the front lines. The prosperity of the Japanese economy during the 1980s was sustained not only by excellent goods, which were developed by diligent technocrats, but also by anonymous employees who connected companies and customers. We must note that information processing skills are far from being fake skills, which are easily connected with irresponsibility.

The following point distinguishes my theory from that of the Aoki school (Marxism on its head). The Aoki school's assertion that Japanese firms solve by the cooperative game and Anglo-American firms solve the same problem as a non-cooperative game possesses no fundamental basis for why Japanese firms can cooperate. Ambiguity and arbitrariness have been regarded as mysterious characteristics of the Japanese, and such characteristics have saved employees from undesirable conflicts. There is no denying that the Aoki school influenced Western researchers, especially in the field of corporate governance, by heightening these prominent propensities of the Japanese.

However, business is the product of rationality. Therefore, if the Japanese had such spurious propensities, then certainly there was no prosperity throughout the 1980s. Meanwhile, rationality never means aggressiveness, and true generosity and sincerity imply shrewd observation and understanding of their customers and colleagues. This is because, as Moore (1902) advocates, good cannot be defined without specifying the situation that one faces. Thus, efficient information processing requires deep intelligence, which is based on social sciences and humanities, although such a virtue is not necessarily nurtured by college education.

It takes long and continuous employment to nurture such skills because, like a natural science, the employment environment should be stable enough to transform experiences into structural knowledge. Entering a firm implies that an employee pledges to abide by the rules of the firm. Accordingly, the employee spends much time mastering such an implicit structure. Economically, this implies that employees invest in themselves and incurred costs are sunk in the sense that they are repayable only if the employee does not leave his firm. On the other hand, employers also wish for long-term employment or her to not waste educational costs.

To summarize, life-time employment is a kind of common sunk-cost investment by an employer and employee to nurture excellent information processing skills. Thus, this convention possesses acute economic rationality. In contrast to my theory, the Aoki school is unable to answer the fundamental question of why the Japanese can cooperate.

Second, the seniority wage system has the following prominent feature. To the extent that an employee does not make a serious mistake, and that he or she is as diligent as others are, he or she can receive a wage equal to those who make remarkable contributions. Such a system has the following economic function that sustains the lifetime employment system: the seniority wage system was implicit insurance against an employee's unintentional failure in business. As discussed above, the lifetime employment system asks an employer for intensive sunk-cost investment, and hence, the employee's wages are reward for this investment. Thus, differing from the ability wage system, which reflects the employee's achievement in the short run, the seniority wage system provides equal returns for the employee's human capital to some extent. This property reduces uncertainty that accompanies human capital investment. With regard to the employee's risk-aversion propensity, the seniority wage system was an ingenious device to enhance human capital investment.

We must note that the human resource function is assigned a more important role than in the wage system, which reflects the short-run performance of employees, because of the difficulty of precisely evaluating an employee's performance. In fact, an employee who is assigned and commits to the human resource function for a long time is a candidate for a future executive. This is because the assessment of the ability and fidelity of each employee is invisible and confidential but is quite important to overcome the typical moral hazard problem of sabotage, which is a peculiar problem in the quasi-fixed wage system. As such, the lifetime employment and seniority wage systems mutually support each other.

Finally, it is a convention that company unions in Japan are organized based on each single company, in contrast to industry unions in the West. While there are few empirical quantitative analyses, this convention was said to have two important functions to prompt economic growth and stability. The first contribution to firm growth is that key people who are promised future executive roles often play important roles in the unions. This fact, although implying compromising behavior by unions, also suggests that executive candidates, including blue-collar workers, could learn the overall structure of their companies. The second function is that, different from industry unions, a company union might make it possible to absorb firm-specific shocks through bilateral negotiations. Under an industry union, it is difficult to absorb exogenous shocks peculiar to a firm by wage negotiation because the inter-firm collective decisions constrain the behavior of a union. Accordingly, the company-union system supported the excellent information-processing and implicit risk-sharing system embedded in the Japanese economy.

1.2.2 From the Plaza Agreement to the Burst Bubble

The average annual GDP growth rate from 1980 to 1985 was 3.3 percent. Including the latter half of the 1970s, this era is called the stable growth decade. Japan enjoyed the most prosperous time that I have experienced. The autonomous economic conventions, discussed in subsection 1.2.1, definitely contributed to this prosperity.

Japan was blessed with stable economic conditions as well as a peaceful political environment. In addition, foreign affairs were a tail wind for the Japanese economy except for trade friction with the US, which owed much to the twin deficits of the US current account and government fiscus.[7] Asian economies such as China and India did not present an economic threat to Japan, and the political order of the Middle Eastern economies, whose crude oil is vital for the Japanese economy, was far more stable than currently. In turn, Japan's excellent labor market properties were refined by this peaceful situation all over the world.

The steady and peaceful progress of the Japanese economy began to fall out of step with the Plaza Agreement of September 1985. The Plaza Agreement was a deal between the G5 (US, UK, Germany, France, and Japan) about coordinated intervention in the foreign exchange market, with the aim of depreciating the USD rapidly. Figure 1.1 illustrates how drastically the JPY appreciated against the USD (articulated from the statistics of the BOJ). Before the Plaza Agreement, the nominal exchange rate fluctuated around 240 JPY/USD, but within only 3 years of the deal, the

Figure 1.1 The exchange rate. *Source*: BOJ Statistics.

JPY appreciated about twice against USD, which meant the exchange rate became 120 JPY/USD.

As background to the global intervention in depreciating the USD in the foreign exchange market, the US recorded a serious current account deficit during the 1980s. This is because the upturn of the US economy owed much to its expansionary fiscal policy accompanying the fiscal deficit. An expansionary fiscal policy increases GDP through the multiplier process and stimulates imports. Thus, a current account deficit and exchange rate appreciation result. In other words, the current account deficit is the other side of the coin of the fiscal deficit. Such a relationship is dubbed the *twin deficits*. From this point of view, the fact that excellent Japanese manufacturing goods were prominently sold in markets was attributed to the loose finances of the US.

However, an accumulating US current account deficit implies that the US economy borrows heavily from foreign economies. Therefore, there is no denying that advanced countries (G5) were quite anxious about the deja vu of the Nixon shock of 1971. The countries were eager to sustain the confidence of the USD, and hence, accepted the reduction of the US's burden. To enforce this agreement, the G5 intervened in the foreign exchange market for the purpose of depreciating the USD.

Nevertheless, for better or worse, since Japan enjoyed its heyday, such a huge amount of loss by the realignment of the exchange rate has not been regarded as a serious concern for most Japanese who are alienated from economics. However, the following unavoidable reality is evident from the effect of the Plaza Agreement. Even under a flexible exchange rate system, regardless of surplus or deficit, a cumulative disequilibrium of the current account is not sustainable or cleared by serious and significant realignment in the exchange rate. Accordingly, the monetary authority and the government should be cautious about the long-run movement of the current account and adjust the domestic economic structure and policies so as to equilibrate the current account.

Rapid appreciation of the JPY generated expectations of a downturn of business because the US is the biggest customer for the Japanese manufacturing industry, and the appreciation triggered a hike of international prices of Japanese manufacturing products. In reality, in 1986, the appreciation of the JPY caused recession. Although the GDP growth rate decelerated, it was only a transition process. As figure 1.2 (Statistics of National Account: Cabinet Office) indicates, it is evident that Japan regained steady growth soon after 1986. Figure 1.3 (BOJ Statistics) suggests that the BOJ's adoption of a sustained low interest policy significantly contributed to the upturn of business.[8]

Such an expansionary monetary policy aimed to hinder the excess appreciation of the JPY. This is because a lower domestic short-run interest rate makes fund management in JPY disadvantageous and results in USD purchases in exchange for the JPY. However, there was an unexpected economic consequence of this defensive monetary policy. Figure 1.4 illustrates the annual growth rate of M2 (BOJ Statistics). We observe that the growth rate of money exceeded not less than 10 percent per annum from 1987 to 1990. The policy, which pegged the call rate at quite a low level, was woven into the expectations of the private sector. In other words, firms and the affluent class of individuals borrowed a huge amount of money from financial

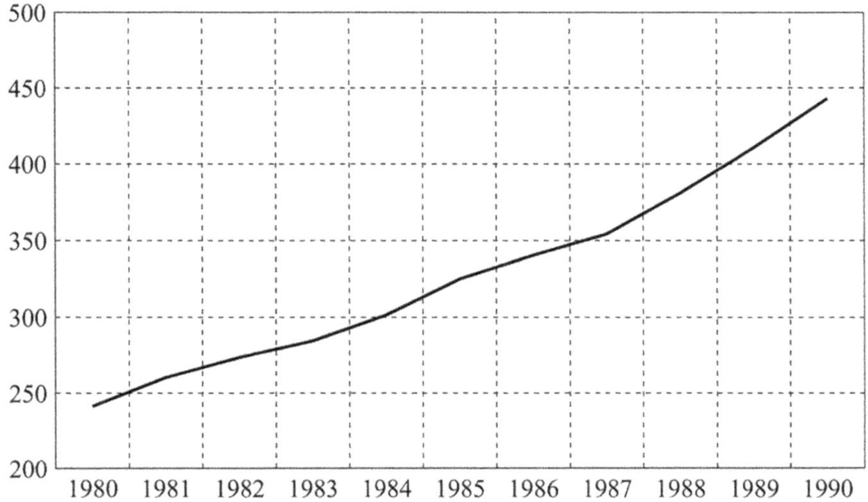

Figure 1.2 The nominal GDP. *Source*: SNA.

Figure 1.3 The call rate. *Source*: BOJ Statistics.

intermediaries to invest in stocks and immobile assets. Such zealous behavior sought unlimited lending by the BOJ to banks because the BOJ committed to peg the call rate at a historically low level. Thus, speculative bubbles emerged.

Moreover, another incident occurred, namely, the origin of speculative bubbles. Based on the prosperity of the 1980s, which relied on the US economy, the retained profits of firms, which are approximately defined by the difference between the sum of business surplus and mixed income, and capital formation (SNA), amounted to JPY 30 trillion per annum until 1989, when people began to become suspicious about future stock and immobile

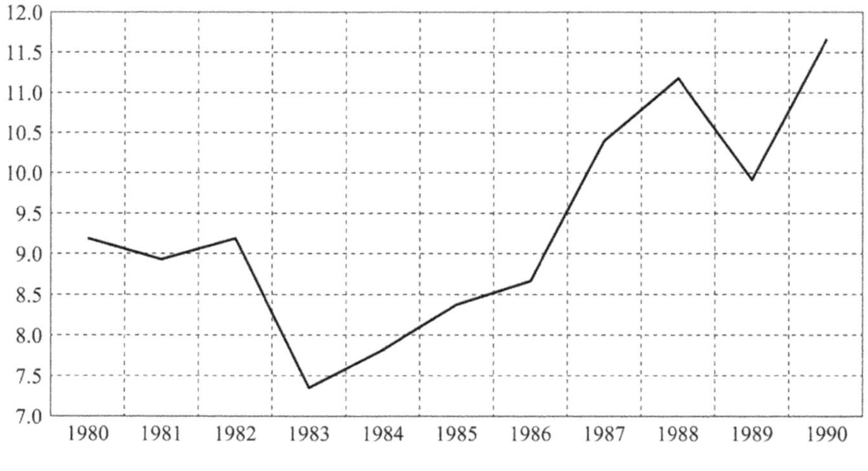

Figure 1.4 Growth rate of money supply. *Source*: BOJ Statistics.

asset market returns. Hence, retained profits increased from JPY 5 trillion to JPY 10 trillion. In summary, Japanese firms held ample liquidity throughout the 1980s.

To capture this business opportunity, financial intermediaries developed new types of investment trusts although they were quite primitive compared with today's sophisticated derivatives, regardless of whether such sophistication is vicious or not. Trusts are classified into two types: *tokkin* (designated pecuniary trust) and *fantora* (fund trust).[9] These derivatives were ultimately reinvested into stocks and immobile assets, and thus played a significant role in boosting the bubble. This phenomenon of firms eagerly speculating in trusts was dubbed *zaiteku* (efficient technology for making money).

The Economic Planning Agency, currently reorganized in the Cabinet Office, reports in its Annual Economic Report of 1993 that the aggregated land price soared by about three times from 1985 to 1990. Accordingly, a round estimation tells us that the annual rate of return for land was

$$\frac{300}{5} = 60 \text{ percent}$$

For example, an individual who bought a condominium for JPY 30 million could obtain

$$30(\text{JPY million}) \times (1 + 0.6) = 48(\text{JPY million}),$$

by selling it 1 year later. The net revenue was 18 million JPY, which amounted to about four times labor income. Considering that the call rate, which was a good proxy of the rate of return for nominal assets, was around 3 percent during this period, this return was astronomically high. Those who succeeded in speculation during the bubble boom obtained incredible capital gains.

What was the situation on the stock market? According to the Nikkei Average, the stock price was JPY 10,000 at the end of 1985 and JPY 39,000 by the end of 1989. While the collapse of the stock market occurred the year before that of the immobile asset market, the rate of return for the stock was almost equal to that for land (i.e., 60 percent) throughout the boom.

Thus, many people made huge amounts of money during the bubble boom. I remember that numerous lucrative residences and buildings emerged and night clubs competed for short-term prosperity. There are still a lot of Japanese who cannot forget such a fanatic time and are bothered by a huge amount of debt, which is a tragic consequence of the bubble boom.

We must note that speculative bubbles are essentially a zero-sum game at least in the long run. This is because there is fundamental value in each asset. In general, a fundamental value is defined as the discounted capitalized value of marginal utility or the revenue stream of an asset. Residences, buildings, and land have value because they provide services: utility derived from comfortable living, and revenue accrued from an efficient business environment. However, expected lifetime income, which corresponds to the discounted present value of human capital, and/or marginal productivity of land, which is equal to the rent in equilibrium prescribe the upper limits of the market price of land. Therefore, if the market prices exceed their fundamental value, speculative bubbles burst sooner or later.[10] As such, the bubble boom was thwarted. I discuss more sophisticated and realistic causes of the bubble boom in the next section.

1.3 THE 1990s AS AN OVERTURE OF THE CRISIS

1.3.1 Why Did the Bubble Expand?

In the previous section, I acknowledge two economic factors that triggered the bubble: the BOJ's uncompromising low-interest policy and the huge accumulation of corporate savings. We must, however, notice that even though speculative motives were urged by economic conditions, such fanatic speculation would not occur unless it resulted in increased earnings. In other words, all speculators considered that their deeds made money, at least ex-ante. This subsection is devoted to exploring the reasons why speculators formed such a belief. This problem is closely related to the massive accumulation of public debt through the 1990s, and hence, it is important to understand the origin of Japan's economic crisis.

The resultant bubble was a consequence of the following financial incentives:

i. moral hazard under limited liability; and
ii. lack of caution about prudential regulation of financial intermediaries

First, let us consider the negative effect of point i. Limited liability is part of a financial contract that provides concession when the net return of a speculation becomes negative. If a debtor neglects the collateral for simplicity, the net return becomes zero when the capital income records a negative. The true purpose of a limited liability contract is to assist the debtor to recover from the excess liability and enable him to live a civilized life. However, speculators in the bubble boom used this part of the financial contract in an illicit way. Many corporations and individuals planned to hide their capital income when they could make money, and when this failed, they did not hesitate to abscond.

Let us consider this illicit behavior with a numerical example. Assume an investment return is:

$$\frac{1}{2}\times 10+\frac{1}{2}\times[-10]=0$$

In this sense, the fundamental value of this asset is zero. However, in the case of a limited liability, the expected return becomes

$$\frac{1}{2}\times 10+\frac{1}{2}\times[0]=5.$$

This fact implies that an asset that has no intrinsic value can possess some positive economic value under the limited liability contract. I define such a phenomenon as a *speculative bubble*. In other words, since the investors can get rid of the downside risk, they take excessive risk from the point of view of the economy in general. I dub these calamities speculative bubbles.[11]

Second, vehement speculation of such bubble assets is prompted by lack of investigation and judgment of financial intermediaries. Japanese financial intermediaries could not determine lenders' would-be non-performing debts, which suggests that they sought friendly industry policies, which were then adopted by the Ministry of Finance (MOF) and termed *Goso Sendan Hoshiki* (Guarded Convoy Procedure). Hence, the Japanese financial intermediaries considered that the MOF ultimately would manage everything even though they had failed at their business, as far as they followed the MOF's order. Such an attitude is directly connected to lack of prudence, as I have pointed out above.[12]

1.3.2 Economic Consequences of the Bubble Burst

We must now consider facts that tend to be overlooked. The bubbly asset, as discussed in subsection 1.3.1, is associated with a negative return, −10, for half of the investors. This is evident from the weak law of large numbers. Such a loss burdens unrelated individuals other than the investors under limited liability.[13] This comprises huge amounts of non-performing debts. Emerging non-performing debt was not undertaken by the private sector, and hence, the public sector was forced to give concessions. The buyout of non-performing debt and injection of public funds into the already weary financial intermediaries are typical examples. In addition to this, enlarged public investment, which amounted to JPY 30 trillion, is an implicit subsidy to industries such as construction, civil engineering, and immobile asset industries, which were heavily impacted by the bursting of the bubble boom. Most of these enlarged government expenditures are financed by the issuance of public debt. Accordingly, the bursting of the bubble is the acute origin of the pathological accumulation of public debt.

Nevertheless, until the Asian financial crisis erupted in 1997, the Japanese economy had enjoyed prosperity despite holding vague anxiety about the huge amounts of non-performing debt. We need to consider why such a restless yet optimistic view prevailed. Two factors supported this ephemeral optimism. First, extravagant capital gains obtained by those who sold stock and land by the collapse of the bubble stimulated aggregate consumption (although such income does not appear in the SNA statistics).

Let us consider this expansionary effect by using the numerical example used in subsection 1.3.1. The increase in income per capita amounts to (1/2) × 10. When we denote the marginal propensity to consume c, the multiplier effect expands income per capita as much as:[14]

$$\frac{1}{2} \times 10 \times \left[c + c^2 + c^3 + \cdots \right] = 5 \times \frac{c}{1-c}. \tag{1.1}$$

Note that this value can be regarded as a realized value, not as an expected value as per the law of large numbers (see appendix C for this theorem).

In addition, the second effect is that implicit subsidies given to fatigued industries, which are discussed in subsection 1.3.1, were financed not by additional tax but by new issuance of public debt. This effect implies that such a roundabout expansionary fiscal policy saved the economy from declining business in exchange for an additional financial burden on future generations.[15] Since speculation in this context is generally a zero-sum game, the corresponding fiscal expenditure, which is equal to the sum of liquidities provided, amounts to (1/2) × 10 per capita. Accordingly, through the multiplier process, additionally created income is as much as:

$$\frac{1}{2} \times 10 \times \frac{1}{1-c} = 5 \times \frac{1}{1-c}. \tag{1.2}$$

It is not much of an exaggeration to say that the expansionary effect brought about by a fiscal-monetary policy that aims to compensate the capital loss from the speculative bubble burst is stronger than that of an increment in aggregate consumption triggered by the expansion of such bubbles. This is evident from a comparison of equations (1.1) and (1.2).

The fact that most Japanese still enjoyed their prosperity until the Asian financial crisis was due to a fiscal-monetary policy that gave concessions to losers of the burst bubble. The acute origin of the pathological public debt accumulation, which bothers the current Japanese economy, stems from the annihilation of fiscal discipline accompanied by expansionary monetary policy in those days.

Let us verify this discussion using actual data. Data are based on BOJ statistics. It is necessary to distinguish actual number from growth rate. Assume that nominal money supply was JPY M and the increasing ratio is g per annum. Then, nominal supply becomes $M[1 + g]$ in the next year. As a result, the increment is g in the growth rate but Mg in the actual number. When M is a large number, the actualized increment of money supply is also quite large, even though g is small. Accordingly, we must be cautious about not only the growth rate but also its actual number.

Figure 1.5 illustrates the increased rate of M2+CD from 1991 to 1998. Except for 1992 when a drastically tight money policy was adopted for bursting the bubble, this rate was around 3 percent per annum. At first glance, one may feel that the BOJ did not follow a prominent expansionary monetary policy.

However, from figure 1.6, which illustrates the time series of stock for money supply (M2+CD), we observe that money supply increased by JPY 110 trillion during the 8 years from 1990 to 1998. When we consider that, as figure 1.6 shows, money supply expanded explosively by 1990, it is evident that the BOJ's monetary policy was quite aggressive during the 1990s. In fact, as indicated in figure 1.7, the call rate (overnight/no collateral) was lowered after the peak of 1991 and was set around 0 percent by 1996, which is the same level as that in the present.

Thus, growth rate and actual number provide different impressions about the assessment of monetary policy because the actual number is a significantly large value. The stock of M2+CD in 1990 (the peak of the bubble boom) already amounted to JPY 500 trillion. For the growth rate of around 3 percent per annum, calculating by a simple rate yields

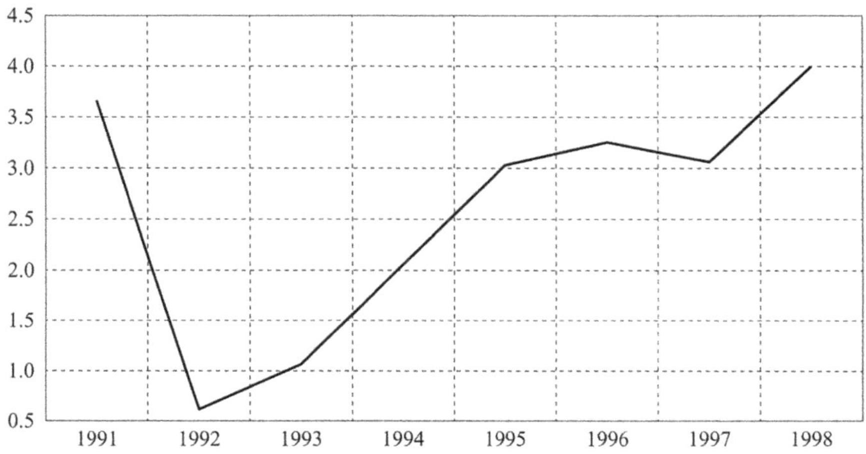

Figure 1.5 The growth rate of money supply. *Source*: BOJ Statistics.

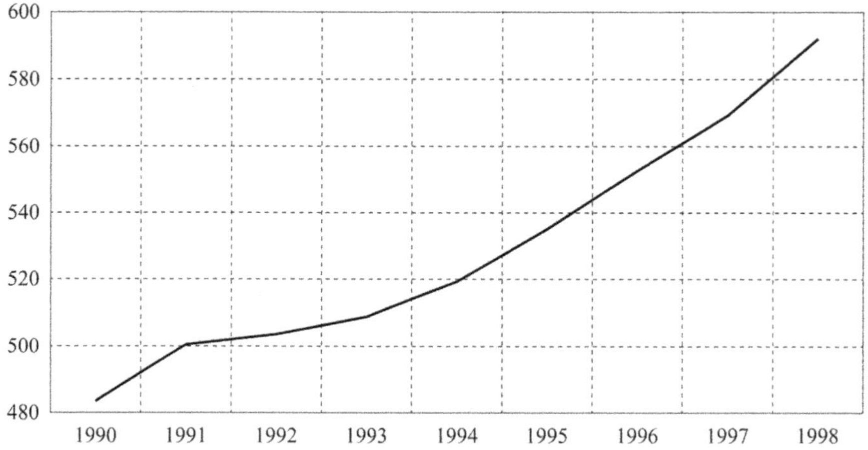

Figure 1.6 Actual number of M2 + CD. *Source*: BOJ Statistics.

$$500 \times [1 + 8 \times 0.03] = 500 \times 1.24 = 620 \text{ (JPY trillion)}.$$

This number is approximately equal to the stock of M2+CD in 1998. Thus, whenever an actual number is higher, we must be cautious about its growth rate and the actual number itself.

In addition, there is a serious pitfall when an analysis focuses only on the growth rate: the threat of compound rate. The simple rate is a first-order approximation of compound rate. Hence, when an analysis is extended over a long period, the high-order effect, which is brought about by the interest of

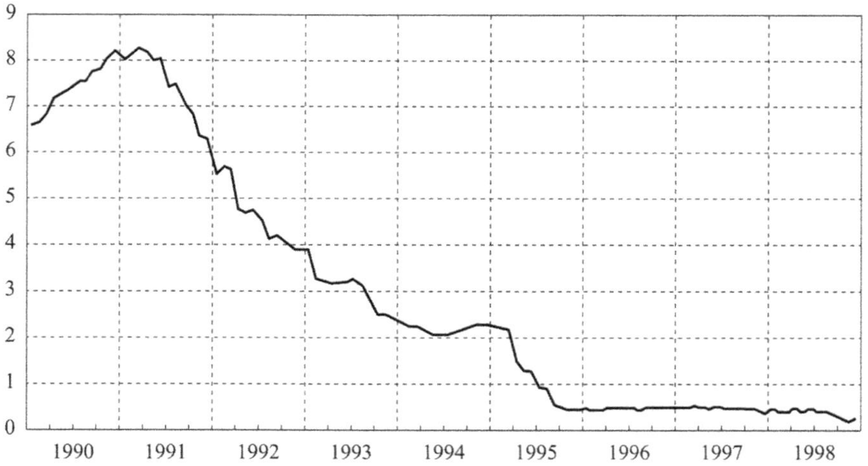

Figure 1.7 The call rate. *Source*: BOJ Statistics.

interest, becomes non-negligible. According to the compound rate calculation, after 10 years, JPY 1 million is valued as:

$$1\times[1+0.1]^{10}\ (\text{JPY million}).$$

Let us calculate this value using the binominal term theorem. When we take the second-order approximation, we obtain:

$$\begin{aligned}1\times[1+0.1]^{10} &\approx 1\times\left[1+{}_{10}C_1\times0.1+{}_{10}C_2(0.1)^2\right] \\ &= 1\times\left[1+1+45\times10^{-2}\right]=1\times2.45=2.45.\end{aligned}\qquad(\text{JPY million})$$

A lay person might apply a simple rate and conclude that such an asset bears 100 percent interest over 10 years. However, when the expiry date is far into the future, the second-order term becomes impossible to neglect: it amounts to JPY 0.45 million. This example suggests that if a researcher concentrates on data's growth rate, his recognition possibly underestimates the reality.

Figure 1.8 illustrates the growth rate of the total debt of the Japanese government (this statistic corresponds to the MOF's statistic, "Current Stock of Public Debt, Borrowing, and Government's Guarantee"; the Cabinet Office (CAO) estimates in the SNA that the general government debt amounted to JPY 1,200 trillion in the 2014 fiscal year). The average growth rate is 8.8 percent when we exclude the ratio of 1991.

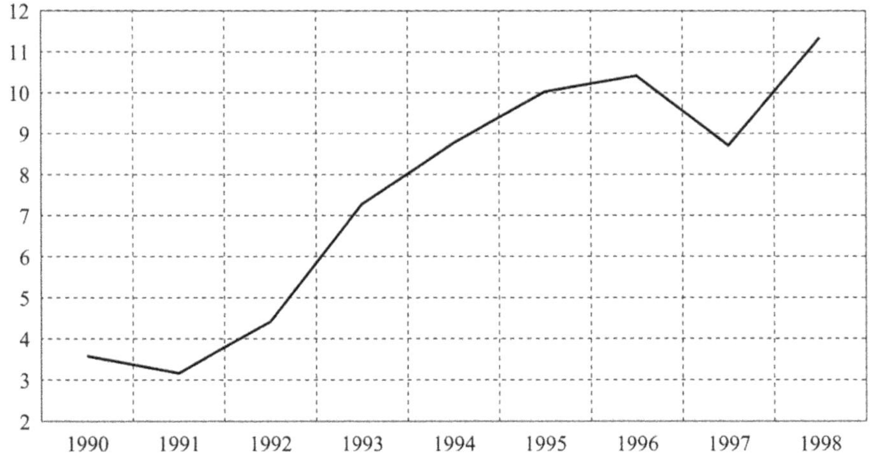

Figure 1.8 Growth rate of public debt. *Source*: BOJ Statistics.

At first glance, one may suspect that the assertion that an extraordinary expansion in public debt occurred in the 1990s is wrong. Nevertheless, figure 1.9 reveals how precarious the threat of compound rate is. During these 8 years, government debt soared. From about JPY 220 trillion in 1990, the debt almost doubled to about JPY 430 trillion in 1998.

In addition, there is a more inclusive conception of money supply: widely defined liquidity. Since the data are limited to recent years, as a proxy, let us observe the time trend of the sum of M2+CD and government debt. This proxy was JPY 720 trillion in 1990 and soared to JPY 1,040 trillion in 1998. The average growth rate was 4.7 percent per annum.

Since such a huge amount of liquidity was injected into the Japanese economy within a short span of 8 years, it brought about two significant expansionary effects from money stock carried over and newly issued money. I first concentrate on the former effect. Remember that the call rate was quite low throughout the years as illustrated in figure 1.7. Such monetary policy provided good opportunities such as changing high-interest loans to low-interest loans and promoting liquidation of non-performing debts. Then, a surplus of funds emerged among financial intermediaries. Money stock cannot be considered as staying idle except for the legal reserve. Accordingly, the surplus was consumed by an increase in capital investment, and thus, income and savings increased owing to the multiplier effect. In other words, a large amount of money stock, in itself, supported the Japanese economy impaired by the burst bubble. The problem was the ambiguity, partly owing to imperfect disclosure and cosmetic accounting, about the amount

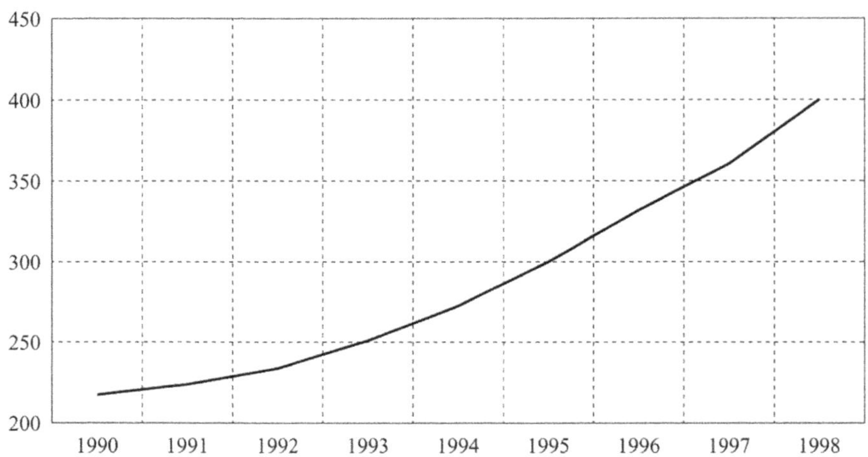

Figure 1.9 Actual number of public debt. *Source*: BOJ Statistics.

of non-performing debt that was hoarded by the financial intermediaries. Throughout the 1990s, the Japanese economy held serious systemic risk in the financial sector.

Second, I study the effect of newly issued public debt brought about by the expansionary fiscal policy whose efficiency as a public good is arguable. When we neglect the negligible small monetarizing cost incurred by public debt, the debt can be regarded as a kind of money that accrues interest (or money as a kind of public debt whose expiry date is infinite and accrues zero interest). Accordingly, the newly issued public debt possesses the same effect as the outstanding monetary stock. Since the increment in the government debt from 1990 to 1998 exceeded JPY 200 trillion as shown in figure 1.9, it had a substantial effect on prosperity, which was dented by the Asian financial crisis.

Figure 1.10 illustrates the growth rate of nominal GDP from 1990 to 1998. Although we observe a −2 percent growth in 1998, the average growth rate was 2.7 percent (the growth rate in 1990, which was the peak of the bubble boom, affected this number: when we omit the rate in 1990, the average growth rate becomes 1.9 percent). In actual numbers, this means that nominal GDP increases to JPY 60 trillion during these 8 years. Thus, it is unnatural to consider that the Japanese economy ceased to prosper coincidentally with the burst of the bubble. Most Japanese enjoyed the sequent prosperity from the 1980s but nevertheless were seriously concerned.

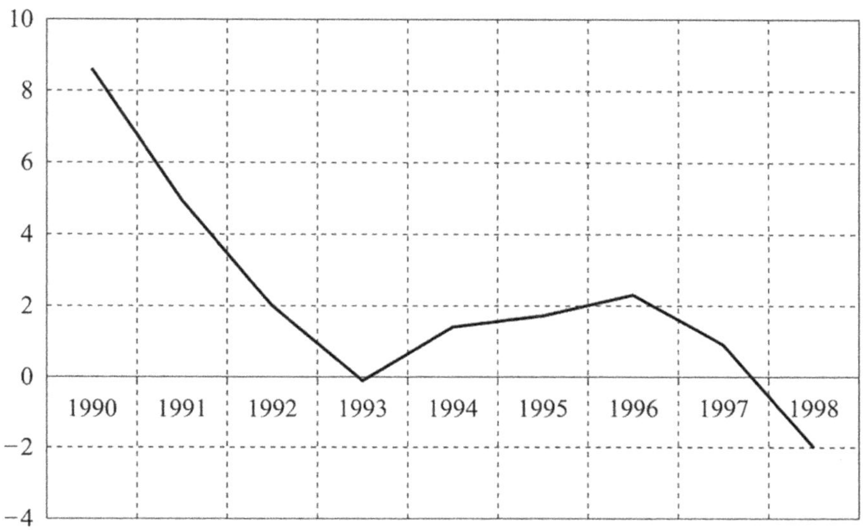

Figure 1.10 Growth rate of nominal GDP. *Source*: SNA.

1.4 REVELATION OF THE CRISIS

Around 1997, many Japanese were anxious about the consequence of the accumulating non-performing debt, the amount of which was still unknowable even to the authorities, although it was not as serious as the present figure. Financial intermediaries' disclosure of non-performing debt was continually delayed, and hence the public aid through the Deposit Insurance Organization (DIO) could not stabilize the economy effectively as such lack of transparency provoked suspicion about the future.[16]

In such an unfortunate situation, a devastating financial shock came from Asia: the Asian financial crisis. This calamity determined the fate of the Japanese economy until today. The Asian financial crisis originated from Thailand and spread to Indonesia, Malaysia, the Philippines, and South Korea. Although it is difficult to determine the causes of this contagious financial shock explicitly, the economies that were affected possessed a common characteristic. They achieved remarkable economic growth during the first half of the 1990s by active invitation of foreign capital. Some of them were dubbed "The East Asian Miracle" by the World Bank.

However, it was necessary to enforce such industrial policy to achieve international confidence about their economies' financial stability as advanced economies wanted to lend money to them as safely as possible. These growing Asian economies pegged their exchange rate against the USD, which is considered the world's most reliable currency. Nonetheless, the pegged exchange rates overestimated the values of their currencies, and hence, were advantageous to imports and disadvantageous to exports. Thus, they were concerned about the structural current account deficit and borrowed heavily from overseas.

One might consider that depreciating the exchange rate would be adequate to resolve this problem. However, regardless of whether the foreign exchange system is the fixed exchange rate system or the gold standard, if an economy sets the exchange rate at an overvalued level, its currency is misunderstood to represent the strong potential of the economy. Accordingly, a devaluation of currency tends to be regarded as a loss of an economy's global image and/or politicians' competance. Thus, the monetary authorities delayed devaluation.[17]

On the other hand, a large part of investors in advanced economies not only financed sound capital investment but also myopically speculated on immobile assets, whose prices were expected to arise in conjunction with economic development. In Thailand, which was the origin of the Asian financial crisis, this tendency was remarkably prominent. As discussed in subsection 1.3.1, speculative bubbles inevitably collapse without exception because of the acute existence of fundamental value. The boom of Thailand's market followed the fate of the speculative bubbles, and prices of land began to fall in early 1997. Foreign investors then withdrew speculative funds from Thailand's domestic financial intermediaries. Accordingly, a huge pressure of conversion from Thailand's baht (THB) to the USD emerged. However, since Thailand did not hold sufficient reserves of the USD, it faced the crisis of depleting its foreign reserve. Thus, Thailand was forced to move from the quasi-fixed exchange rate system to a flexible exchange rate regime. As a result, a rapid depreciation of the THB to the USD ensued. Thai domestic financial intermediaries, which speculated in immobile assets in THB could not repay their debts in USD, and many of them went bankrupt. Needless to say, the Thai economy experienced a serious stagnation.

Other Asian economies pursued a similar policy in the sense that they pegged the exchange rate at an overvalued level against the USD to obtain global confidence in their economy and invite affluent foreign capital. Consequently, suspicion about the economies' repayment ability was provoked, and foreign funds canceled loans simultaneously. Thus, the financial turbulence that originated in Thailand spread to many East Asian economies.

The Asian financial crisis heavily impaired the Japanese economy. As discussed at the start of this subsection, the Japanese economy held many ambiguities about the amount of non-performing debt owing to insufficient disclosure, especially in the financial sector. The crisis brought forth these ambiguities. It is notable that fatigued major financial intermediaries such as Yamaichi Securities, the Long-Term Credit Bank of Japan (Nihon Choki Shinyo Ginko), Nippon Credit Bank (Nippon Saiken Shinyo Ginko), and Hokkaido Takushoku Bank went into bankruptcy. Since the Japanese economy had not experienced such large-scale bankruptcy after World War II, this nemesis aggravated the long-term expectations of the non-financial sector and households and curtailed aggregate consumption and capital investment. Nominal GDP, which hit the ceiling in 1997 (JPY 520 trillion), decreased to about JPY 19 trillion (−1.9 percent per annum). The Japanese economy took 10 years thereafter to regain the same level of GDP. In this sense, it seems plausible that we should regard 1997 or 1998 as the substantial burst of the bubble, not 1990 or 1991.

1.5 THE JAPANESE ECONOMY IN THE 21ST CENTURY

1.5.1 Compromise between Keynesianism and Neoliberalism: Theoretical Background

There is a substantial rift between Keynes's thinking and that of American Keynesians. Keynes was a sympathizer of the Liberal Party and he wrote many articles in related magazines. Keynes's concept of freedom is in line with the traditional British concept of freedom in the sense that human beings cannot live without society, and hence, there is some moral to which every person should submit. Such thinking admits freedom as a measure for self-realization under constraint of the moral because there are common interests, which is the origin of a society and should transcend private myopic wants. As discussed throughout Part II, stability of a monetary economy belongs to this category. Collective decisions are unavoidable while managing such common interests because an individual's decentralized decisions do not always reflect such interests. Existence of a government and central bank are typical examples.

Keynes's thinking decisively influenced the political stance of the US government. However, the American Keynesians were fascinated by the effectiveness of economic planning rather than Keynes's liberal thinking. A large econometric model, in which Keynes disbelieved, was intensively developed using computers, and the prediction by the estimated model significantly affected the political-economic decisions of the government. There were scarce human elements in American Keynesian thinking. Moore's work (1902), which Keynes loved and was profoundly affected by, advocated that the concept of "good" cannot be defined without specifying the situation. The econometric model of American Keynesianism regarded an economy as an inorganic system. Liberal and affluent contexts included in Keynes's writings vanished, and economics and technology became alike.

Nevertheless, a turning point came with the Vietnam War. Until then, the US economy had been steadily growing, and almost all data were upward sloping. Hence, spurious correlation between them produced good estimation and prediction. However, growth of the US economy decelerated in the 1960s, macroeconomic data began to oscillate irregularly, and as a result, large econometric models exhibited only poor performance.

A landslide conversion of economists from Keynesianism to monetarism occurred following the advent of Milton Friedman, regarded as one of the originators of neoliberalism. Friedman's (1968) vertical Phillips curve hypothesis, which implied that monetary policy matters only when people's expectations contain some misunderstandings, was quite influential for US economists.

In addition, time series analysis, which discarded the estimation for structural equations and focused on the precision of prediction, became popular. Sims (1972) used this method and found that a change in nominal money supply in the US did not necessarily cause a change in nominal GNP in the sense of Granger-Sims causality. The paper was regarded as the evidence of the validity of monetarism. Lucas (1972) asserted that a unique equilibrium price function exists in the two-period overlapping-generations model with uncertainty, whose property supports the quantity theory of money. Otaki (2015a) pointed out the incompleteness of his proof.

As Allen (1931) suggests, it is not unnatural that a hedonism juxtaposes cruelty in a devastating society that experiences a war. This is the acute source of neoliberalism, which neglects the morals and empathy that sustain a society. Friedman and Friedman (1983) is a typically articulated book that advances neoliberalism.

It seems that compromise has been achieved between the new Keynesians and monetarists in the sense that money matters in the short run owing to the exogenous stickiness of prices while the quantity theory of money is upheld in the long run. Accordingly, there has been little substantial theoretical progress in the prevailing macroeconomics after Lucas (1972).

1.5.2 Did Structural Reform by the Koizumi Administration Prompt Coordination Failure?

The deep recession accompanied by the Asian financial crisis changed the Japanese way of thinking. Inadequacy and delay in the disclosure of non-performing loans caused the financial bubble to burst and raised questions about the behavior of the government and firms. As discussed in subsection 1.2.1, intensive and efficient information processing skills were considered one of the most outstanding properties of Japanese firms. However, this idea was debunked completely by the Asian financial crisis. Efficient information processing required overlaps between jobs because information sharing supported by communication abilities is necessary. The new way of thinking regards these blurred job boundaries as a cause of irresponsibility, which prevents disclosures and delays the formation of solutions for any difficulties firms face. Consequently, managers have begun to consider the importance of clear job descriptions and boundaries to make employees work more responsibly.

Nevertheless, this idea might require some caution. According to Coase (1937), an organization such as a firm exists because it provides an efficient solution that market mechanisms cannot induce. If a firm exists only with uniform quality of labor and capital, and prices are the only information used by management, then anybody can establish a firm simply by purchasing labor and capital from the market. This is because the contribution of each production input is completely decomposable. However, reality does not support this way of thinking. In general, the performance of a firm depends on how well teams are organized since jobs within a firm overlap and if one part of the firm is idle, it brings disruptions to others and might reduce overall production efficiency. In other words, jobs within a firm are intrinsically inseparable.

Market mechanisms achieve the most efficient allocation when the contributions to the final product can be completely attributable to each production input. In other words, a meritocratic assessment of employees is possible only when performance of an employee does not affect that of other employees. Accordingly, prompting competition among employees by isolating them from each other does not improve overall performance of a firm. The real problem is the confusion surrounding the difference between information sharing within a firm and good corporate governance, which includes clear disclosure to the public.

Clearly, employees become closer to one another when there is intense information production and sharing within a firm. This may trigger a conflict between good corporate governance and firm efficiency. The realignment that took place after the bubble boom is a typical example.

When employees face an environment that can be described as cut-throat competition, there is less information sharing in light of intense employee competition. When employees are isolated like this, the production efficiency of a firm is affected. In other words, *coordination failure* becomes prominent (i.e., when employees are isolated and do not take into consideration how their actions affect other employees, the overall activity of a firm is lowered.)[18]

Soon after entering the twenty-first century, the structural reform implemented by the Koizumi administration unequivocally declared a wide range of deregulation policies to prompt competition. In other words, the newly enacted policies aimed to dismantle the collusive relationships that are pervasive in Japanese society, and attempted to benefit the Japanese economy by reducing vested interests through increased fair competition.

One of the most persuasive reasons why the Japanese society accepted such neoliberal policy actions is because many Japanese agreed with the view that long stagnation prevailed due to collusive relationships between the government and firms.

For example, the Employment Security Law (Shokugyo Antei Ho) and the Dispatched Worker Law (Haken Rodosha Ho) were revised to prompt competition between employees. In 2003, regular employees occupied about 90 percent of the total number of employees. However, this ratio decreased to 60 percent in 2013 (Labor Force Survey, Statistics Bureau, Ministry of Internal Affairs and Communications). There is a significant annual wage differential between regular workers and temporary workers of JPY 2 million (male, 40-years-old, high school graduate: Basic Survey on Wage Structure, Ministry of Health, Labor and Welfare). As discussed in the next subsection on FDI, such a drastic increase in temporary workers was due to the invisible but cheap and abundant labor force in East Asia rather than to increased competition between domestic employees.

In 2000, the Large-scale Retail Store Law (Daikibo Kouri Tenpo Ho) was abolished. This law aimed to protect small retailers against large retailers, which have overwhelmingly large sales floor areas. Japanese politicians regarded these existing small retailers as evidence of inefficiency of the Japanese economy, and hence, to vitalize regional cities, they felt it was necessary to prompt the entry of large retailers and increase competition.

However, we observed the tragic consequence of this abolishment in almost all regional cities. Most commercial streets, which were composed of small retailers, were devastated. Instead, roads to large shops like shopping mall located in suburbs were improved and most residents chose to shop there instead. Thus, the core of the cities was hollowed. When we take into consideration the community function of cities, this phenomenon is problematic. The concept of *efficiency* as understood by advocates of structural reform is defined too narrowly. It is worthwhile reconsidering what exactly is included in the concept of efficiency.

As discussed above, structural reform, which went unchanged despite the temporary change in the ruling party, is based on neoliberal thinking. Neoliberalism is far removed from liberalism. Liberalism requires morals that are necessary for maintaining social cohesion. By contrast, neoliberalism ignores such morals and justifies intense competition, which does not take into consideration the losers' impoverishment or the cost to society. We note that such harsh competition is not assumed in economic theory. There is a significant rift between the concept of competition in economic theory and in reality.

1.5.3 Surge of Foreign Direct Investment and Economic Hollowing

The labor market deregulation described in the previous subsection strengthened the employers' right to terminate employees, de facto. That is, since non-regular workers are substitutable when an expiration date arrives, deregulation facilitated the easy adjustment of the employment level. I provide an example of the adjustment process as follows.

Suppose a firm build a factory overseas. The firm waits for regular workers to retire and fills those vacancies with non-regular workers. When this employment policy reaches substantial implementation, the company closes the factory easily by moving the rest of the regular employees to another factory. Thus, the labor market deregulation enhances FDI, which aims to use the cheap and abundant labor force in East Asia. This tendency became prominent around the turn of the century.

A rough estimation of the total amount of FDI is derived in the following way. According to the National Accounts of Japan (SNA), capital investment was almost unchanged from 2005 to 2014, which amounted to JPY 70 trillion. The Basic Survey on Overseas Business Activities (BSOBA, Ministry of Economy, Trade, and Industry) shows that the ratio of FDI to domestic capital investment rose from 20 percent in 2005 to 30 percent in 2014. Accordingly, about JPY 7 trillion per annum flowed overseas. This shows the significant domestic investment opportunities that were lost by the surge in FDI.

The surge not only decreased aggregate demand through the multiplier effect but also reduced employment opportunities, especially for non-regular workers. Both effects undermined business and prolonged economic stagnation. I define this phenomenon as *economic hollowing*.[19]

One might argue that FDI benefits the Japanese economy through significantly higher profits while FDI curtails domestic labor demand. This assertion is logically consistent, but in reality, the average profit rate of overseas affiliates was 4.7 percent from 2007 to 2014 (manufacturing industry: Corporation Industry Statistics, Ministry of Finance) while the rate for the domestic manufacturing industry was 4.1 percent (BSOBA). The difference is subtle, and we can at least note that FDI is not as profitable as it may seem.

Furthermore, there is a serious problem in the surge of FDI: volatility of the exchange rate. In East Asia, economic transactions are cleared mostly in Chinese yuan, and the currency is pegged to the USD. For simplicity, let us assume that all transactions are cleared in USD. When an overseas affiliate remits its earnings to its headquarters in Japan, the exchange rate is not affected by the remittance and the firm can enjoy the advantage of a cheap labor force in East Asia because its remittance is small relative to the overall scale of the foreign exchange market and does not affect the exchange rate. However, this outcome no longer holds when every overseas affiliate of FDI firms simultaneously remits its earnings. Since huge amounts of JPY are purchased in exchange for USD earnings, the JPY significantly appreciates against the USD. Such an appreciation provokes capital losses derived from the appreciation. This is a typical example of a *fallacy of composition* in the sense that a principle that is valid for one economic agent cannot be applied to an overall economy.

Thus, regardless of the original intent, remittance to headquarters in Japan is hindered by the appreciation of the JPY. The exchange rate appreciated about 3 percent per annum against the USD (BOJ Statistics). As mentioned above, the BSOBA showed a profit rate to total sales of 4.7 percent per annum. Accordingly, the profit rate in JPY is

$$4.7 - 3 = 1.7(\text{percent}).$$

In such a situation, foreign affiliates hesitate to send remittances to their headquarters in Japan. According to the BSOBA, retained profits of foreign affiliates are significantly higher than those of domestic affiliates. Since retained profits are defined as the difference between gross profits and the sum of dividend and tax payment, retained profit is the amount of money that is newly accumulated within the firm. Thus, the trend outlined above suggests that remittances are hindered by the expectation of exchange rate appreciation.

To summarize, I have clarified that the profit rate of foreign affiliates to total sales is not significantly different from that of domestic affiliates, and that the expectation of JPY appreciation caused by huge remittances becomes an obstacle. Accordingly, earnings from FDI do not sufficiently enrich the Japanese economy. Thus, it is plausible that the negative aspects of FDI as discussed above (i.e., economic hollowing) dominate earnings from FDI and FDI can be regarded as one of the most serious causes of prolonged stagnation.[20]

Economic hollowing is a type of *coordination failure*. In general, coordination failure is provoked by dysfunction in the government and/or senior business management. Economic hollowing is a peculiar problem of a monetary economy. As we discuss in Part II, whenever people believe in the intrinsic value of money, the price level becomes fixed and the shortage of aggregate demand immediately leads to contraction in aggregate supply and an increase in unemployment. Therefore, FDI not only reduces domestic capital investment but also discourages household consumption owing to curtailed labor income. In this respect, FDI causes the economy to stagnate. On the other hand, profits earned overseas cannot be remitted at face value because such remittances cause an appreciation of the JPY. Consequently, contractionary effects possibly dominate expansionary effects derived from FDI earnings.

However, one might argue that the surge of FDI involves a huge amount of sunk cost and since overseas affiliates at least earn normal profits, it would be almost unfeasible to cease FDI. This argument is persuasive to some extent. Nevertheless, I propose that we focus on the future economic structure and not the past. If we accelerate capital investments overseas, more investment costs will be sunk and remittance of profits obtained from these additional investments will be even more difficult because of the accelerated JPY appreciation. I advocate for the creation of an organization composed of the public and private sector to harmonize domestic capital investments and FDI strategically. In addition, I urgently recommend the reallocation of factories to domestic regional cities, which are suffering from rapid and serious population outflow.[21]

1.5.4 Fiscal and Monetary Policy in the Historically Low Interest Era

In the previous subsection, I focused on effects of labor market deregulation to the overall economy and emphasized that neoliberalism supports major deregulation. This subsection deals with the fiscal and monetary policies from the structural reform era to the present.

Throughout these years, aggregate demand management policy was based on textbook Keynesian economics, that is, in a manner in which authorities did not consider any side effects of the policies. As discussed in more depth in Part II, a monetary economy fails to achieve the first best allocation without wise government support.

On the contrary, neoliberal thought, which was the most important mantra of structural reform, prompts cut-throat competition and attempts to remove obstacles that hinder the functions of market mechanisms. Since cut-throat competition lowers equilibrium prices enough to create new demand, an aggregate demand management policy is unnecessary. In this sense, there was a serious rift between the ideas in macroeconomic and microeconomic policy.

How did the Japanese government reconcile this rift? One must remember the political slogan that was frequently used during the structural reform: move resources from the public sector to the private sector. Whenever a part of the public sector is privatized, that entity earns more in the short run. This outcome is because public organizations are not allowed to pursue profit maximization, and instead are meant to enhance economic welfare at least on paper. It does not imply that privatization is always wrong. Since maximization of economic welfare is vague, the public sector tends to lack discipline unless constituents exercise sufficient oversight.

However, privatization cannot solve everything. For example, urban redevelopment and reconstruction of important infrastructure require wise collective decision making. When the provision of such public goods is inefficient, privatization is not necessarily the right solution. In other words, the economy and culture cannot be revitalized only by profit motives. Deregulation of the floor area ratio enforced by structural reform meant that the government left an important part of urban planning to the private sector. Such deregulation substantially meant a massive transfer of public space to the private sector. Benefits from deregulation emerged as capital gain from land, and possibly enhanced aggregate demand. Nevertheless, when high-rise buildings loom irregularly, there is no denying that deregulation led to a disordered view of metropolitan cities. It is questionable whether deregulation was effective in improving economic well-being except through a fiscal expansionary effect.

As such, some deregulation policies in microeconomics are closely related to an expansionary aggregate demand management policy. In this sense, economic policies from structural reform are based on a compromise between neoliberalists and Keynesians. Neoliberals compromise with Keynesians by asserting that aggregate demand management is necessary to stabilize an economy.

Such deregulation of the labor market aimed to assure the flexibility and competitiveness of the labor market by permitting various worker categories, which could be interpreted as expansionary aggregate demand management. However the great recession, which was beyond the control of Japan, was provoked in 2008. The Japanese economy, which was recovering from the Asian financial crisis, decelerated yet again. According to the SNA, employee income was curtailed by JPY 11 trillion from 2008 to 2009, and private consumption and nominal GDP fell by JPY 10 trillion and JPY 30 trillion, respectively. Nominal GDP in 2014 was JPY 480 trillion compared to JPY 510 trillion in 2007.

To summarize, a compromised Keynesian thought is regarded as the leading principle of Japanese fiscal and monetary policy. As illustrated in figure 1.11, the penetrating and historical low interest policy can be interpreted as an attempt to stimulate consumption and capital investments although it did not perform as well as expected. We must note, meanwhile, that a low interest issuance of public debt implies a high market price of public debt. Since the majority of public debt is held by domestic financial intermediaries, a high valuation of public debt raises their asset values and contributes to sustaining sound business.

To enforce such a drastic price maintenance policy under the pressure of a high fiscal deficit, the BOJ was obliged to radically increase the purchase of public debt. The ultimate manifestation of this kind of aggressive monetary policy was the radical quantitative easing (QE) policy (Ijigen Kinyuu Seisaku) under the second Abe administration from 2012.[22] It is evident from figure 1.12 that M2 money supply increased by JPY 100 trillion within only 3 years of 2012.

This radical QE policy annihilated fiscal discipline because the government borrowed huge amounts of cheap money. In reality, as illustrated in

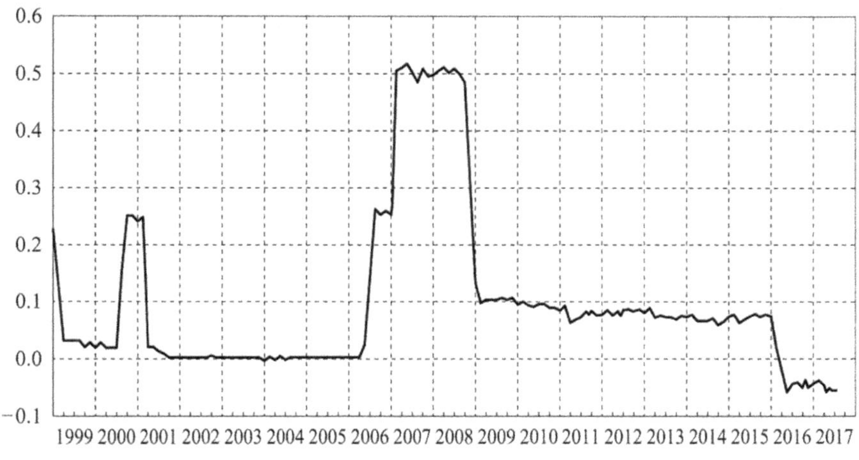

Figure 1.11 The call rate. *Source*: BOJ Statistics.

Figure 1.12 Actual number of M2. *Source*: BOJ Statistics.

figure 1.13, the stock of public debt exponentially increased from JPY 450 trillion in 1998 to 1050 trillion in 2015. Expansion of social security expenditure owing to the rapid aging of the population is regarded as the direct cause.

Since public debt is convertible to the extent that people believe in a nation's levying ability, not all debt might be redeemed. However, the current Japanese economy holds huge amounts of public debt of about 2.5 times its GDP, and this number is seemingly approaching a level beyond the levying ability of the government. Once debt holders become suspicious about the

Figure 1.13 The actual number of public debt. *Source*: BOJ Statistics.

government's ability to repay public debt, the price of public debt falls violently, and this could possibly trigger financial panic. Accordingly, an urgent recommendation is to reduce the stock of public debt.

Tax hikes are unavoidable for the redemption of public debt. When the tax increase is burdened onto the same generation as the issuance of public debt through a lump-sum tax, no additional burden is left for subsequent generations (Ricardian equivalence theorem). However, in the critical situation that the Japanese economy faces, a tax burden associated with the redemption hangs over future generations. Accordingly, it is not self-evident whether the tax hike for the redemption is neutral or not. We must consider which of the following two effects dominates: (a) an expansionary effect by which a huge amount of redemption enriches the previous generation, and (b) a contractionary effect to aggregate consumption of the current generation, which is caused by the decrease in disposable income due to the tax increase. Let us calculate which of these two effects dominates (see chapter 3 for a more rigorous discussion).

Let us denote the value of the redemption to the old generation, which is equal to the tax increment accruing from the young generation as, ΔT. In addition, change in real GDP compared with before the issuance is denoted by Δy. Then from the equilibrium condition of the aggregated goods market, we obtain

$$\Delta y = c\left[\Delta y - \Delta T\right]. \tag{1.3}$$

We must note that the additional tax revenue cancels out the redemption of public debt. When we solve equation (1.3) on Δy, we can ascertain that the following holds:

$$\Delta y = -\frac{c}{1-c}\Delta T \Leftrightarrow \Delta y - \Delta T = -\frac{\Delta T}{1-c}. \tag{1.4}$$

Equation (1.4) advocates that disposable income is harshly reduced by the redemption of public debt. This fact implies that issuance of public debt inevitably burdens descendants.

Therefore, judging from the intergenerational equity perspective, issuance of public debt is not recommended. When we apply an interpretation of neoliberalism, which asserts that one never needs to consider others' interests in pursuing one's own interests, to intergenerational problems, this means that a specific generation does not need to take the interests of their descendants into consideration. In this sense, we find that the current radical aggregate demand management policies, which are based on new Keynesian theory, compromise neoliberalism.

1.5.5 Why Is Inflation Not Provoked?: Farewell to the Quantity Theory of Money

It is surprising that the political slogan that attempted to ease deflation eroded rapidly. Some provocative articles asserted that the current Japanese economy and that in the Showa Depression in 1930 were alike, and that the economy would sink toward bottomless stagnation.

According to the Long-term Economic Statistics (Institute of Economic Research: Hitotsubashi University), the consumer price index fell by 20 percent from 1929 to 1931. How does this compare with the current Japanese economy? The inflation rate defined by the consumer price index (Statistics Bureau of the Ministry of Internal Affairs and Communications) was 1.8 percent in the 1980s, 1.0 percent in the 1990s, and –0.3 percent in the 2000s (10-year averages). It is apparent that the severity of the current sequential disinflation is quite different from that in the Showa Depression. Furthermore, the economic causes that triggered the disinflation and deflation are quite different.

The most distinct point is the difference in the foreign exchange system. The Showa Depression was aggravated by the gold standard. By contrast, the present system is a flexible exchange rate system based on fiat currencies. The Showa Depression was triggered by the ripple effect of the Great Depression in the US in 1929. The US was the largest customer of Japanese goods, of which the main export was silk-related goods. The Great Depression decimated demand for Japanese exports, and hence the current account recorded a huge deficit, which provoked an outflow of gold.

Consequently, extreme and rapid contraction of credit occurred. Banks hastened repayment of their outstanding loans, and as a result, silk-related industries such as textile and agriculture were forced to sell their products at low prices to finance repayment. Numerous non-financial corporations and banks went into bankruptcy. Thus, the Japanese economy experienced rapid deflation and fell into bottomless stagnation. In other words, as we explicitly analyze in chapter 5, the intrinsic value of money is determined by the depth of belief in the value of money, and the fierce deflation in the Showa Depression was triggered by a strengthened belief in the value of gold, which sustained the gold standard.

The Japanese economy in the twenty-first century faces a completely different situation: Sufficient or excess liquidity is provided in the economy; and therefore, a flexible exchange rate system guarantees that the exchange rate adjusts to equilibrate the current account at least in the long run. In addition, Japan is free from the fear of running out of funds for import clearance owing to its abundant foreign reserves. Thus, the current economic situation is completely different from that of the Showa Depression.

Then why has inflation not been caused despite the intention of monetary authorities? There are two crucial factors. First, as discussed in subsection 1.5.2, neoliberal business management, which plays down the inseparability of jobs, provoked coordination failure within firms. Labor productivity stagnation reflects this fact. According to the Japanese Productivity Center, nominal labor productivity stagnated or even fell around the turn of the century. As we analyze more precisely in chapter 4, curtailed labor productivity implies the contraction of potential production capacity, and hence, the equilibrium condition of the aggregate goods market requires that consumption should be suppressed instead of increased in money demand. Eventually, disinflation and/or mild deflation occur to raise the rate of return for money.

Second, the Japanese still believe in the intrinsic value of the JPY despite historically slack financial conditions. I regard a state in which people no longer believe in the intrinsic value of money as the quantity theory of money holds. Using a mathematical expression, the quantity theory of money can be written as

$$p_t = \frac{M_t}{\kappa}, \ \kappa \text{ is a positive constant.} \tag{1.5}$$

where M_t is nominal money supply and p_t is the price level. According to this thinking, money does not possess an intrinsic value and an additional increase in money supply is entirely absorbed by a proportional change in the price level. In other words, no matter how money supply is increased, the purchasing power of money is invariant at κ. Ascribing to this line of thought, one cannot understand the current macroeconomic situation of the Japanese economy. It should be noted that new Keynesians, who constitute the mainstream in macroeconomic theory, assume this hypothesis at least in the long run (appendix B summarizes the new Keynesian theory).

In Part II, I show that, by excluding the quantity theoretic equilibrium price function as in equation (1.5), a rational expectations equilibrium (REE) can be constructed with an assumption that if one has sufficient money, everyone can purchase any amount of goods at the market price. In such an REE, monetary expansion (in the sense of widely defined liquidity) enforces additional savings. To create these savings, disinflation and/or deflation must be caused, because money carried over should be used to purchase more future goods.

To summarize, the following are the two dominant economic factors that prescribe movement of price level:

i. labor productivity stagnation; and
ii. huge increase in nominal money supply in the sense of widely defined liquidity under the unwavering belief in the intrinsic value of money

However, it is necessary to highlight that there is a limit to the belief in the intrinsic value of money. In particular, when the nominal stock of money greatly exceeds potential production ability, people become suspicious about the exchangeability of money for goods. In such a calamity, the quantity theory of money revives, and uncontrollable high inflation might be triggered.

In reality, the Japanese economy suffered from hyperinflation from 1973 to 1974.[23] Since sound policies were implemented at that time, the Japanese economy managed to overcome the crisis. Nevertheless, the current economy has accumulated far more than JPY 1,000 trillion in public debt. The majority of Japanese bank deposits are used to finance public debt. Accordingly, an urgent political topic is the avoidance of hyperinflation and/or massive default of public debt, because this will inevitably cause serious political unrest owing to the emergence of severe income disparity among the population. As discussed above, the following economic policies are urgently recommended.

i. Expansion of fiscal expenditure, including social security, should be curtailed.
ii. Redemption of public debt should be advanced in preparation for the aging society.
iii. Substantial tax hikes are inevitable to enforce (i) and (ii).

Although these scenarios may seem unacceptable, their advantages in allowing the Japanese economy to avoid hyperinflation are important to consider.

1.6 CONCLUDING REMARKS

I have overviewed Japanese economic history from the 1980s to the present in this chapter. Obtained results are as follows.

First, information processing skills were intensively nurtured and functioned in the 1980s. Such skills created new domestic and world markets through the development of many articulated goods. Since information processing skills genuinely possess positive externalities, efficient internalization is vital for excellent business. Japanese employment practice, which was an implicit insurance system for intensive sunk-cost investment, accelerated skills accrual because it takes a long time to have various experiences and to understand their structural implications. In addition, Japanese prosperity relied on the facts that China and India were not a threat to Japan in those days and that aggressive fiscal policy in the US economy provided good business opportunities for Japanese industry.

Second, in the middle of the 1980s, abundant earnings from overseas markets and the penetrating low interest policy of the BOJ, which aimed to decelerate rapid appreciation of the JPY, laid the basis for the feverish speculative bubble from the late 1980s to the early 1990s. In other words, serious economic problems in the US crucially affected the emergence of the speculative bubble.

Third, morally hazardous behavior that stemmed from the MOF's excessively forbearing industrial policy toward domestic financial intermediaries and the accommodative monetary policy conducted by the BOJ were the direct cause of the bubble boom. Domestic financial intermediaries could borrow unlimited money from the BOJ at a low interest rate and simultaneously wove the MOF's policy into their business. They *rationally* anticipated that they would be rescued to the extent that they were in good faith with the MOF even though speculative investment failed. As such, speculative bubbles are generated by irresponsible attitudes toward downside risks in an essentially zero-sum game. Accordingly, the bursting of the bubble boom was a natural consequence. In reality, the regulation about lending to immobile assets enforced by the MOF and the acute contractionary monetary policy terminated the bubble boom.

Fourth, until the Asian financial crisis in 1997, many Japanese enjoyed consecutive years of prosperity supported by the radical and expansionary fiscal policy. In this sense, the expression "the lost decade" is not a truism. Improper accumulation of public debt, which is a challenge for the current Japanese economy, originated in this era. Huge amounts of money were poured into the economy to compensate for devastating loss arising from the bursting of the bubble throughout the 1990s.

Fifth, the Asian financial crisis decisively changed the way of thinking of the Japanese. They regarded the outgoing Japanese economic system that put much importance on the power of organization as old fashioned. In addition, they considered that the inside of an organization is hardly comprehensive to outsiders and lacks transparency. Such ambiguity caused delays in dissolving serious economic problems (e.g., non-performing debt), and thereby hindered economic recovery from a long period of stagnation. In this sense, it was a natural consequence that neoliberal thought rapidly came to prevail. The structural reform enforced by the Koizumi administration was in line with this thought. This nexus of policies based on neoliberal thought emphasized overwhelming dominance of self-interested decisions over social cohesion. The aftermath has been devastating. The surge of FDI caused by myopic and disorderly self-centered decisions provoked grievous income disparity among workers and prominent decline in local cities. Despite these appalling consequences and changes in administration, economists' land-slide conversion to neoliberalism has never ceased.

Finally, we should note that illicit compromise has been upheld between neoliberalism and new Keynesianism. Neoliberalists admit the need for aggregate demand management policies. A typical example is the radical QE policy conducted by the Abe administration. Although such a policy seems sophisticated and/or complicated at first glance, the principle is quite simple: annihilation of fiscal discipline. A tremendous increase in social security expenditure caused by aging and a prominent birth rate decline has forced the government to issue huge amounts of public debt. The BOJ *legally* accepts additional issues at face value. This is the reality of the radical QE policy. On the same point, new Keynesians compromise with neoliberalists. As discussed in more detail in chapter 3, the issuance of public debt burdens future generations that will be in charge of redemption. Therefore, new Keynesians are never concerned about intergenerational ethics, and thus are located along the same line as neoliberalists. It is an acute crisis in Japan that most intellectuals are alienated from the concept of social cohesion.

NOTES

1. I remember a reviewer's comment made at the time a paper was accepted by a US academic journal. The study criticized the argument that stable employment does not necessarily imply high efficiency of the Japanese economy. The reviewer commented that he or she could not believe that the Japanese economy was inefficient relative to the US economy. Thus, "common sense" is variable.

2. I am ashamed that I considered active fiscal policy was necessary to sustain the economy and publicly advocated this policy. However, an esteemed professor of our university phoned me and remonstrated my policy stance. He considered it absurd that huge amounts of public money were spent on wasteful investment, giving an array of examples, and he predicted that the fury of citizens would be provoked when they realized the folly of such a policy. His anxiety is persuasive, especially retrospectively given the current fiscal condition, in which public debt has soared to JPY 1,300 trillion. However, to the best of my knowledge, no other academic researcher foresaw this devastating economic situation 20 years ago.

3. For more detail on the theoretical consequences of FDI under a flexible exchange rate, see Otaki (2015a, ch. 9).

4. I purchased a personal computer (PC) in 1988 for the first time. The internet did not exist, at least in Japan, and thus even contact by e-mail was impossible. The PC's main memory was only 640KB, which is unthinkable by present standards. I envied a friend of mine, who had ample research funds, for extending memory via an extension hard disk. Conversely, PCs were quite expensive. My PC was about JPY 400,000 (3,500 USD at the then exchange rate). I first used e-mail in 1996, although such contact was limited to intra-PC. It took much longer to be able to use e-mail by cell phone. Today, it is a global standard that submissions and reviewers' replies in academic journals use the internet. However, such a convenient tool became popular only around the

turn of the century. Before that, airmail had been the vehicle for communication. Graduate school students would await airmail containing reviewers' reports with great anticipation.

5. For more detail, see Aoki (1980, 1988). Fukao and Otaki (1993) criticized the Japanese employment convention for not necessarily being efficient based on a theoretical model.

6. One might consider that more than half of employees are high-school graduates, and alienated from such sciences, and that it is too much of exaggeration to regard most of college graduates as having skills in what they studied. Nevertheless, the rules of firms and experience in reality have given them discipline. Moreover, an excellent entrepreneur is a de facto skillful scientist. Keynes (1936, 14) asserts that employees are unconsciously more reasonable economists than the classical school. Dewey (1916) advocates how experience is transformed into knowledge and/or skills. He writes that "Work which remains permeated the play with the attitude is art—in quality if not in conventional designation" (206).

7. The twin deficits follow the line of thought that the government fiscal deficit causes the deficit of the current account. When we consider the overall economy, the following identity holds:

$$S - I \equiv E - X$$

where the left-hand side represents the difference between aggregate savings and investment and the right-hand side implies a current account surplus (i.e., the difference of aggregate exports and imports).

8. It should be noted that the call rate, which was the policy variable of the BOJ, is unknowable until 1985 from the publicized data. The BOJ adjusted the supply of high-powered money to settle the call rate at a targeted rate.

9. *Tokkin,* an acronym for *tokutei kinsen shintaku,* by which, in exchange for a commission fee, trust banks delivered earnings from their financial investment to the principals, which consisted almost entirely of non-financial corporations. The *tokkin* differs from the *fantora*, an acronym of *fando torasuto,* by which customers can designate the contents of the portfolio of a trust. However, there was much arbitrariness in the contract between the principal (non-financial corporation) and agency (trust bank), and using such mal-property, substantial concessions were made for large investors when serious capital losses of the trusts were realized during the bubble boom. This unequal deal became a serious social problem.

The *fantora* is the common name for *shitei-kin-gai shintaku* (a non-designated trust). While customers designate a range of financial reinvestment to trust banks, they are permitted to organize their portfolios at their discretion within the designated range. In addition, differing from *tokkin,* earnings from the investment cannot be monetized and delivered in kind.

10. A similar argument is upheld on stock price. The fundamental value is defined as the discounted sum of the marginal productivity of capital.

11. Stiglitz (1969) and Stiglitz and Weiss (1981) are the pioneer works of the application of Jensen's inequality.

12. *Goso Sendan Hoshiki* (Guarded Convoy Procedure) comes from the experience of World War II. Freighters and tankers, which carried necessary goods to the

front line, were guarded by destroyers and light aircraft carriers. Battleships guarded a convoy in harmony with the most inferior ship. In turn, the phrase came to direct the fact that the MOF (battleship) gave the most favorable concession to the most inefficient financial intermediary (freighter or tanker).

13. According to the law of large numbers, when investors approach a large number, the probability (a kind of possibility) of success converges to the frequency of success.

14. Chapter 2 provides a dynamic microeconomic foundation for the multiplier effect, which is found by Kahn (1931) on an increase in employment volume. Keynes (1936) transforms the employment multiplier to the fiscal multiplier, which is familiar to us. Otaki (2016b) clarifies the relationship between the two multipliers.

15. The theory extended in chapter 3 deals with the process from the emergence of speculative bubbles to the accumulation of public debt.

16. Public aid means public finance through the DIO that aims to prompt the depreciation of non-performing debts accumulated within the financial sector. According to Kamakura (2005), the Japanese government prepared JPY 58 trillion for the guarantee in the 2005 fiscal year. From this budget, the DIO used no less than JPY 40 trillion.

17. The gold standard is composed of two international agreements: (1) attendees pledge to fix their parities against gold; and (2) monetary authorities pledge currency convertibility into gold at any time. This system is based on the confidence in gold's intrinsic value. As discussed in Part II, money never circulates without confidence. Advocates of the gold standard consider that gold is more reliable to guarantee the intrinsic value of a currency than the levying ability of an economy, which is an alternative guarantee of currency, because supply of gold is inelastic and gold possesses a value as a treasure in itself.

The Showa Depression in Japan (1930) originated from the extreme decline in sales of products of the silk-related industry whose biggest customer was the US. The Great Depression was triggered in 1929 soon after Japan's return to the gold standard. Japan suffered a serious current account deficit from the devastating decline of the silk-related industry, which was Japan's flagship export industry. A current account deficit immediately implies contraction of money and credit because gold flows out of the country. Private banks were obliged to ask borrowers to collect loans. This resulted in shortage of operating funds of non-financial industries and triggered a devastating chain of bankruptcy involving many private banks.

18. For more details on the supply-side inefficiency brought about by the Structural reform, see Horiuchi and Otaki (2017, ch. 5).

19. For a more detailed theoretical analysis of FDI in a monetary economy, see Otaki (2015a, ch. 9).

20. This logic is an application of the isolation effect under a flexible exchange rate system, which originates from Laursen and Metzler (1950). For a more precise discussion, see Otaki (2015a, ch. 9).

21. I note that while there is some similarity between what I am advocating and US president Donald Trump's assertion that economic policies should prioritize US economic interests, Trump in fact was threatening multinational enterprises to

increase employment opportunities in the US. However, I oppose his quick use of military threats and arbitrary economic sanctions, which goes counter to the principle of democracy. I believe that such socialization of capital investments can never be achieved without fair and intelligent discussion. In addition, Keynes often proposed that capital investments should be socialized to stabilize volatile economic fluctuations. For example, see Keynes (1936, ch. 12).

22. A negative interest policy was implemented from 2016. The BOJ provided 0.1 percent interest on excess reserves until 2008, although accruing interest in the excess reserve was allowed for an exceptional case by the Law of the Bank of Japan. Private banks deposited money with the BOJ as a consequence of the QE policy. The 0.1 percent interest rate exceeded the market rate of public debts and abundance in retained profits of non-financial industries hindered additional lending by private banks. The interest rate of excess reserves attracted private banks and idle money concentrated in the reserve deposit. As a result, the excess reserve's interest rate, instead of the call rate, became a policy variable of the BOJ.

In 2016, a negative interest rate was imposed on a part of the excess reserve. By the interest arbitrage between excess reserves and public debts, the interest rates of public bonds also became negative, which implied that the market price of the bonds exceeded their face value. The negative interest policy was aimed at increasing bank lending to non-financial industries. The achievement is, nevertheless, quite arguable.

23. The hyperinflation was dubbed "the insane prices" (Kyoran Bukka). Radical expansionary fiscal and monetary policies undertaken by the Tanaka administration tightened the demand and supply relationship in the goods market. Unfortunately, this coincided with the first oil crisis. These calamities provoked suspicion about the availability of supply of goods. The consumer price index rose by 12 percent in 1973 and 23 percent in 1974.

Part II

THEORY

Chapter 2

A Conundrum in Monetary Economics

Does Keynes Abandon the Second Postulate of Classical Economics?

ABSTRACT

This chapter examines how an idle production resource such as involuntary unemployment is provoked. Traditional Keynesian theory, which includes menu cost theory, violates the second postulate of the classical school. It should be noted, however, that Keynes extends that postulate rather than denying it. I show that price stickiness assumption is unnecessary but that the separation of aggregate demand from supply is vital. The problem of double coincidence of wants establishes such a separation. By deploying an OLG model with money, this chapter clarifies how involuntary unemployment is caused under the flexible price assumption.

2.1 INTRODUCTION

Many economists consider that the second postulate of classical economics, which asserts that the marginal disutility of labor is equalized to the real wage, should be abandoned to induce the existence of idle production resources (i.e., involuntary unemployment). The traditional Keynesian approach assumes that significant costs for realignment make the nominal wage insensitive to a change in the price level. Since this school regards that the price level is determined to equilibrate the goods market, the price level rises along with an autonomous increase in the aggregate demand. Accordingly, the real wage falls and thus labor demand increases. However, to the extent that the second postulate is not abandoned, such a reduction in the real wage discourages the aggregate labor supply. Thus, there is a contradiction and the second postulate should be discarded to show the existence of involuntary unemployment.

In the context of the menu cost theory, which originates from Blanchard and Kiyotaki (1989), traditional Keynesian theory can be interpreted as positing a substantial menu cost exists in the renegotiation of the nominal wage. As I shall show in section 2.2, the same property emerges as that in Blanchard and Kiyotaki (1989) if such a menu cost in the nominal wage negotiation exists (note that the price-staggering model in Gali (2008) implicitly assumes that prohibitive menu costs are incurred when a firm revises its offer price in a disorderly fashion).

In other words, this fact implies that menu cost theory belongs to the same category as traditional Keynesian theory in its exogenous introduction of a price stickiness assumption. Consequently, both theories violate the second postulate of the classical school.

In contrast to the traditional Keynesian theory including menu cost theory, Keynes (1936) emphasizes that a reduction in the nominal wage is only associated with a proportionate fall in the price level, and thus is neutral to the equilibrium employment level. His logic is as follows: According to elementary economics, the employment level is determined by the level at which marginal cost (product of the nominal wage and the inverse production function) is equal to marginal revenue (output price); hence, if the output price hike is proportionate to the nominal wage, the employment level is kept unchanged because the real wage is unaffected.[1]

How does this assertion of Keynes relate to the second postulate of the classical theory? According to Keynes (1936, 14–15)

> whereas they [workers] do not resist reductions of real wages, which are associated with increases in aggregate employment and leave relative money-wages unchanged, unless the reduction proceeds so far as to threaten a reduction of the real wage below the marginal utility of the existing volume of employment.

To summarize, Keynes realizes that workers are willing to work as long as the real wage exceeds the marginal disutility. Therefore, he admits that when the real wage is located above the labor supply curve (marginal disutility curve), every worker prefers to work rather than be unemployed. In this sense, Keynes does not dismiss the second postulate of the classical school but extends it. I will discuss this issue in detail in section 2.3.

If we admit the aforementioned fact, we can ascertain that the incentive to promote labor supply, which comprises the supply side of an economy, does not become an obstacle to establishing a theory of effective demand. The true and deep problem is how to separate decisions concerning aggregate savings and capital investments. If one succeeds in inducing a capital investment schedule that is independent of households' saving decision, the fiscal multiplier process is rebuilt on a rigorous microeconomic foundation.

Nevertheless, it is not as facile as it seems at first glance. Traditional capital investment theory (e.g., see Uzawa [1968]) presumes that the objective function is the market value of a representative firm. As I will show in section 2.4, in such a setting, capital investment by a firm is equivalent to a household's surrogated savings. This fact implies aggregate savings and capital investments are two sides of the same coin and that introduction of the investment function in addition to the savings function never means the segregation of such decisions.

From another perspective, saving is the demand for future goods in exchange for present goods. Therefore, to achieve such a separation of decisions, it is sufficient to introduce, as a theoretical construct, an economic agent whose objective in an economic activity differs from the saving decision (i.e., demand for present goods in exchange for future goods). We need not stick to traditional capital investment, whose objective function is not suitable for this purpose.

The two-period overlapping-generations model (OLG model) with money is the simplest measure for describing the separation because money is a proxy for future consumption opportunities. In an OLG model, the younger generation wants future goods in exchange for producing current goods. In contrast, the older generation needs current goods. There is the serious problem of double coincidence of wants. Such a problem arises from the segregation between the demand/supply decisions for current goods in an economy. To the extent that money is recognized as equivalent to future consumption, the dysfunction is eliminated. Consequently, the theory of effective demand is sustainable only in monetary economic theory.

As will be discussed in section 2.5, however, there is another conundrum in establishing the theory of effective demand: assessment of the relevance of the quantity theory of money. Whether or not monetarism, which alleges that the movement in price is proportionate to the nominal money supply, is upheld is vital to exhibit the existence of idle production resources. This is because an economy always achieves full-employment equilibrium if the current price can fall arbitrarily to clear an excess supply in the current goods market as assumed in the quantity theory of money.

Lucas (1972) alleged that he proved that the quantity theory of money holds in a two-period OLG model. However, as Otaki (2015, 177–90) elucidates, his assumptions are quite restrictive and the proof in his stochastic version is invalid. As will be shown in section 2.5, there are multiple equilibria in the OLG model for a production economy, which is a well-known property of a pure exchange economy.

Regardless of whether the economy in question includes a production process or not, such multiplicity or indeterminacy is peculiar to monetary economics. This property comes from the tautology that money possesses an economic value because people believe in its intrinsic value; that is, if people become skeptical about the future value of money, they tend to avoid money hoarding and increase consumption in the current period. This leads to a hike in consumption and the current price level, which implies the depreciation of the current value of money. Thus, the current value of money, which by definition is equal to the inverse of the current price level, is determined by rational expectations concerning its future value.

This stringent fact also indicates that there is no guarantee that the current price level is determined at the level that clears the labor and goods market. Unemployment is provoked whenever individuals hold disbelief in the intrinsic value of money because serious disbelief causes a price hike and reduces the real cash balance significantly (here, it must be noted that the real cash balance is always equal to the real expenditure of the old generation). The discussion above asserts that effective demand theory, which is proposed by Keynes (1936), is hardly tenable without the existence of money.

This chapter is organized as follows. Section 2.2 recasts traditional Keynesian theory as an application of the menu cost theory. Such an articulation implies that there is no substantial progress made by the incumbent new Keynesian theory over the traditional Keynesian theory in the sense that some exogenous price stickiness assumption is unavoidable for obtaining Keynes-flavored results. Section 2.3 clarifies the fact that Keynes (1936) does not dismiss the prescription of labor-supply incentive in the second postulate of classical economics. His extension of the second postulate confirms that the distortion in the labor market such as realignment costs for the nominal wage (a kind of menu cost) has no relation with the theory of effective demand.

Eventually, we find that the separation between saving and capital investment decisions is vital for proving the existence of idle production resources. Section 2.4 reexamines whether the introduction of the investment function provides a meaningful solution on this question, as Uzawa (1968) suggests. I show that the investment function does not demarcate the saving-investment decision to the extent that a firm behaves as a maximizer of its market value, which is a standard assumption in Tobin's (1969) q theory. This is because capital investment corresponds to the surrogated savings of individuals in such an assumption.

In section 2.5, I provide an alternative viewpoint concerning the theory of effective demand. If the aggregate demand comprises not only the consumption of income earners but also income-independent consumption (e.g., consumption of annuity receivers), the aggregate saving (income minus income earners' consumption) decision is segregated from expenditure decision (income-independent consumption). Thus, it is proved that the two-period OLG is a convenient way of describing Keynesian economics. In conjunction with the endogenous price stickiness peculiar to monetary economy, I complete the full description of a mathematical model of the theory of effective demand in section 2.6. Section 2.7 provides some meaningful concluding remarks.

2.2 TRADITIONAL KEYNESIAN THEORY AS A MENU COST THEORY

This section expresses traditional Keynesian theory as an application of the menu cost theory. I assume that the goods market is under perfect competition, and the labor market is characterized by worker's monopsony. That is, the equilibrium of the labor market is described as a Stackelberg equilibrium in which a worker is a leader and an entrepreneur is a follower.

By assumption, an entrepreneur maximizes his profits for a given real wage, W/p, where W denotes the nominal wage and p is the price level. The profit maximization condition is

$$f'(L)=\frac{W}{p}, \tag{2.1}$$

where L is the employment level and f is a strictly concave production function. Let the inverse function of equation (2.1) be denoted as

$$L=\lambda\left(\frac{W}{p}\right). \tag{2.2}$$

A representative worker maximizes his utility subject to equation (2.2). That is,

$$\max_{W} U\left(\frac{W}{p}\right) \equiv \max_{W}\left[\frac{W}{p}\cdot\lambda\left(\frac{W}{p}\right)-G\left(\lambda\left(\frac{W}{p}\right)\right)\right], \tag{2.3}$$

where G is a strictly convex and twice differentiable function that represents the disutility of labor. The solution must satisfy

$$\frac{W}{p}=\frac{G'(L)}{1-\eta^{-1}}, \eta \equiv -\frac{dL/L}{d\left[\frac{W}{p}\right]/\left[\frac{W}{p}\right]}, \tag{2.4}$$

where η is the elasticity of labor demand to the real wage. Equation (2.4) is the modified second postulate of the classical school. Since a representative worker has monopsonic power, he or she weaves how the real wage falls along with providing additional labor at the nominal wage negotiation. Accordingly, as is indicated in equation (2.4), total labor supply is curtailed, when compared with the case of perfect competition.

Let us define the aggregate demand, y.

$$y \equiv c(y) + \frac{I}{p}, \tag{2.5}$$

where $c(y)$ is the aggregate consumption and I denotes the nominal independent expenditure. The equilibrium of the overall economy is illustrated by figure 2.1. Curve L^DL^D is the labor demand curve that corresponds to equation (2.2). Curve L^SL^S is the labor supply curve that is defined by equation (2.4). The intersection E_L is the equilibrium of the labor market unless menu cost exists.

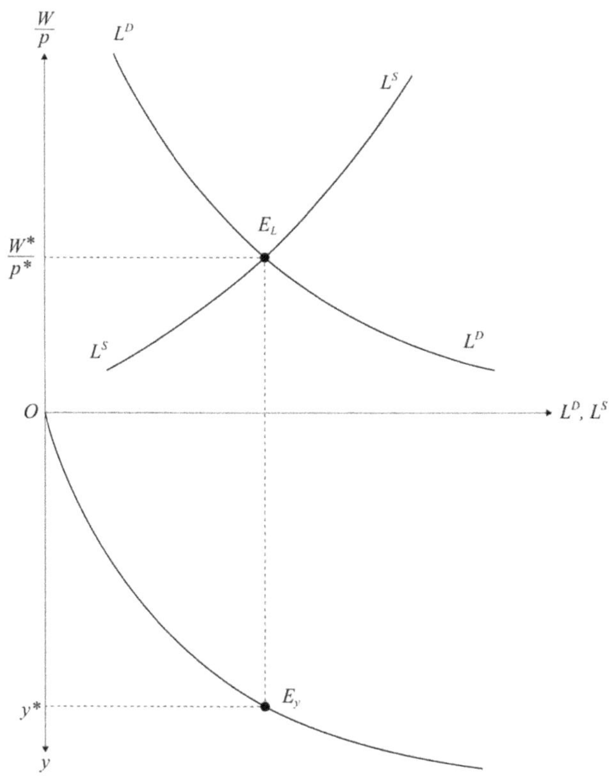

Figure 2.1 Classical macroeconomic equilibrium. *Source*: Author.

The aggregate supply is achieved at point E_y in the fourth quadrant, and thus, the price level that equalizes both sides of equation (2.5) is determined.

Let us denote equilibrium prices by (p^*, W^*). As per the envelope theorem, when the nominal independent expenditure increases by ΔI, the welfare loss, ΔU, caused by keeping the nominal wage unchanged is

$$\begin{aligned}\Delta U &= \frac{1}{2}U''\left(\frac{W^*}{p^*}\right)\cdot\left[\left[\frac{p^*}{p^{**}}-1\right]\frac{W^*}{p^*}\right]^2 + o\left(\left[\Delta W^*\right]^2\right) \\ &= \frac{1}{2}U''(\cdot)\cdot\left[\frac{W^*}{p^*W^{**}}\right]^2\cdot\left[\Delta W^*\right]^2 + o\left(\left[\Delta W^*\right]^2\right) < 0,\end{aligned} \tag{2.6}$$

where ΔW^* is an optimal change in the nominal wage that is associated with an increase in the independent nominal expenditure ΔI. (p^{**}, W^{**}) represent the optimal pricing after the expansion in the aggregate demand in case there is no menu cost.

Since (ΔI, ΔW^*) belong to the same order, the nominal change is kept intact to the extent that there is a second-order infinitesimal realignment cost for the nominal wage.

In such a scenario, a small increase in the nominal autonomous expenditure causes a hike in the price level, leaving the nominal wage unchanged. Therefore, the real wage is lowered and employment level is improved. This is the same logic as traditional Keynesian theory in the sense of presuming exogenously some degree of price stickiness. This fact implies that there are few insights in menu cost theory about the microeconomic foundation of Keynesian economics.

2.3 IS THE SECOND POSTULATE ABANDONED?

As discussed in the introduction, it is plausible to regard Keynes (1936) extending the second postulate rather than abandoning it. Otaki (2016b) argues that if the real wage is higher than the marginal disutility of labor, every worker wishes to work more. This assertion implies that the upper domain of the labor supply curve is incentive compatible with the participation decision as illustrated by the shaded area in figure 2.2.

Figure 2.3 illustrates the equilibrium of the overall economy. Assume, for simplicity, that the nominal independent expenditure, I, is proportionate to the price level and $I \equiv p \cdot i$ holds, where i is the constant real independent expenditure. The first quadrant in figure 2.3 depicts how the equilibrium of the goods market is achieved. The intersection of the aggregate production function, $y = f(L)$, and the aggregate demand function in equation (2.5) expresses the equilibrium of the goods market. The fourth quadrant illustrates the equilibrium of the labor market. For an *arbitrarily* fixed nominal wage $\bar{W}$, equilibrium is achieved at point E^U on the labor demand curve. This is because, as aforementioned, a combination such as $\left(L^U, p^U_{\bar{W}}\right)$ is located above the labor supply curve and hence the incentive compatibility for participation decision is satisfied. In this sense, unemployment is always *involuntary* if it exists.

Figure 2.3 clarifies the following important property: even though the nominal wage is reduced, this only results in the proportionate decrease in the price level. Thus, there is no change in figure 2.3. This fact corresponds to Keynes's (1936) assertion that the reduction of the nominal wage causes no consequence other than a proportionate decrease in the price level.

Ultimately, we find that incentive compatibility concerning labor supply, which relates to the question whether Keynes abandons the second postulate, is not an essential problem for proving the existence of involuntary unemployment. Meanwhile, what is important is to insert a wedge between the saving and capital investment decision. This is an acute problem that we must solve.

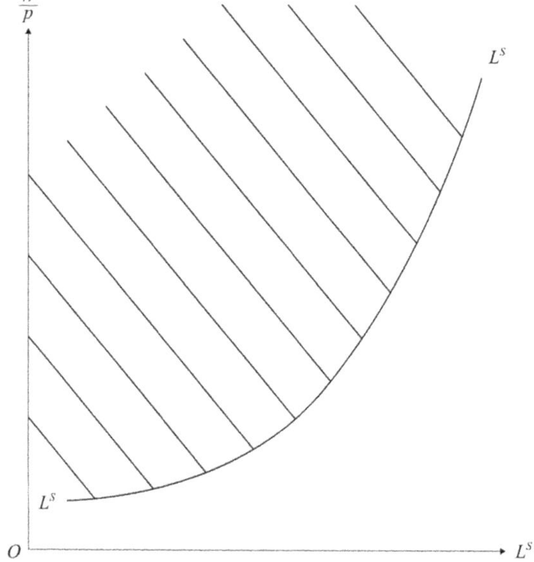

Figure 2.2 Incentive compatibility of labor supply. *Source*: Author.

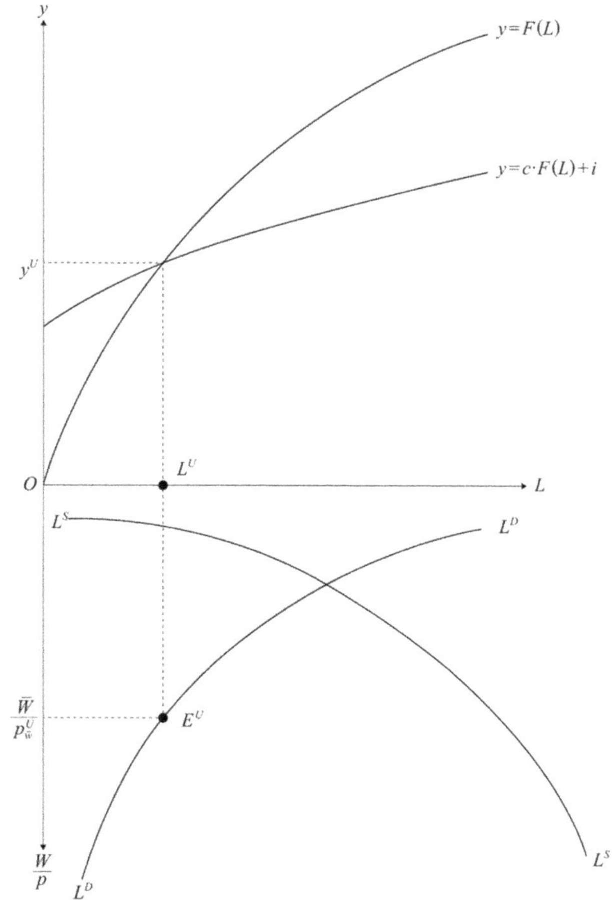

Figure 2.3 Keynesian equilibrium. *Source*: Author.

2.4 THE SEPARATION OF SAVING AND INVESTMENT DECISIONS: DOES INVESTMENT FUNCTION SOLVE THE CONUNDRUM IN MONETARY ECONOMICS?

It is a plausible conjecture that the problem above can be easily dissolved by introducing a rational investment function into the model. Nevertheless, the problem is not so elementary. In this section, I show that investment function based on q theory, which originates from Uzawa (1968), does not succeed in describing the separation of the saving and investment decision.[2]

As a first step, let us analyze the equilibrium condition for the stock market. Let us denote the market value of the representative firm by V_t. The equilibrium condition is

$$\rho V_t = \left[f\left(n^*\right) - wn^* - \varphi\left(g\right) \right] K_t + \dot{V}_t, n^* \equiv \arg\max_n \left[f\left(n\right) - wn \right], \quad (2.7)$$

where ρ denotes the time preference rate, and n is the labor/capital ratio. $f(\cdot)K$ is the aggregate production function. w is the real wage in terms of goods. $\varphi(K)$ is an adjustment cost function, where $g \equiv \dot{K}_t / K_t$ is the ratio of capital accumulation. The budget constraint of the representative individual is

$$y_t = f\left(n^*\right) K_t = wn^* K_t + \rho V_t = c_t + \dot{V}_t, \quad (2.8)$$

where y_t, c_t are the real income and the real consumption, respectively. Substituting equation (2.8) into equation (2.7) and rearranging terms, we obtain

$$f\left(n^*\right) K_t = c_t + \varphi\left(K\right) \varphi\left(g\right) K_t \Rightarrow \dot{V}_t = \varphi\left(g\right) K_t, \forall g, K_t. \quad (2.9)$$

Equation (2.9) is vital. This equation implies that insofar as the value of a firm is determined rationally in the stock market, saving decision is the other side of the same coin of capital investment decision. This result is not unnatural when we consider that the market value maximization of a firm is most beneficial for individuals (i.e., stockholders).

To clarify this discussion, let us consider the following optimal growth problem as a typical example: maximize $\int_0^{+\infty} c_t e^{-\rho t} dt$ subject to equation (2.7) and $\dot{K}_t = gK_t$. The corresponding Hamiltonian is[3]

$$H \equiv \left[f\left(n^*\right) - wn^* \right] K_t + wN_t^* - \varphi\left(g\right) K_t + q_t g K_t. \quad (2.10)$$

This optimal decision problem expresses that a representative individual whose instantaneous utility is the linear function $u(c_t) \equiv c_t$ maximizes his lifetime utility on the capital accumulation path, g, for given returns for production resources: capital and labor. In this description, the representative firm behaves as merely a *static* maximizer of its profits. The necessary conditions for optimality are

$$\begin{aligned} \dot{q}_t^* &= \left[\rho - g^* \right] q_t^* - \left[f\left(n^*\right) - wn^* - \varphi\left(g^*\right) \right], \\ \varphi'\left(g^*\right) &= q_t^* \end{aligned} \quad (2.11)$$

It is not difficult to show that the only stable path, which satisfies equations in (2.11), should be $\dot{q}_t^* = 0, \forall t$. Accordingly, we obtain

$$\varphi'\left(g^{*}\right)=\frac{f\left(n^{*}\right)-wn^{*}-\varphi'\left(g^{*}\right)}{\rho-g^{*}}. \tag{2.12}$$

Equation (2.12) is the same formula as the one obtained by Uzawa (1968). The fact is that the path of optimal capital accumulation is invariant by altering the agent in charge of capital accumulation from firm to individuals to the extent that Uzawa's formula (2.12) holds. Combining this result with equation (2.9), we can ascertain that introduction of q theory to a model cannot separate the capital investment decision from the optimal saving plan. In other words, as far as the stock price is rationally determined, Say's law in the sense that capital investment is surrogated saving is still kept despite the definable investment function. Consequently, the conundrum cannot be dissolved by such an approach.[4]

In addition, this drawback appears in the indeterminacy of the equilibrium nominal real wage, w. The model in section 2.3 can determine the real wage for a given nominal wage because the aggregate demand function is definable independent of aggregate supply function. Nevertheless, in the model of this section, the aggregate demand cannot be discriminated from aggregate supply. When the real reservation wage is sufficiently small, the incentive compatible real wage becomes arbitrary, and thus the level of aggregate supply is not uniquely definable as well as the optimal investment-saving path. In other words, in a general equilibrium growth theory, which is based on q theory, the aggregate supply autonomously increases when the real wage is reduced and vice versa. This is the other evidence that Say's law holds in this type of theory.

2.5 INTRINSIC VALUE OF MONEY AND THEORY OF EFFECTIVE DEMAND

In section 2.4, we observed that the well-defined and q theory–based investment function is unable to demarcate between saving and capital investment decisions. This is because there is no difference in the objective of economic activity of the individual and firm. Both of them prepare for future consumption in exchange for current goods. However, on the other hand, a model that contains the real independent expenditure should be dynamic since savings are the supply of current goods and demand for future goods. In this sense, new Keynesian models such as those discussed in section 2.2 are genetically static and hence not suitable for proof of the existence of idle production resources without somewhat ad hoc price stickiness assumptions.

The key to dissolve the conundrum is the introduction of the *difficulty of double coincidence of wants* into theory that generates a monetary economy.

In my context, those who save want future goods in exchange for current goods. Accordingly, an economic agent who wants current goods but possesses no future goods should exist in a model. If transactions occur between these economic agents, the aggregate expenditure of the latter type of agents (those who prefer current-goods) becomes independent of aggregate savings.

A sufficient condition for sustaining such transactions is *confidence* in the value of money. It is evident that the transaction between agents whose type of want differs does not become self-conclusive in the sense that an agent who receives money in exchange for his goods *rationally* waits for other transaction opportunities so he can purchase his preferred goods. Thus, the transaction within potential difficulty of double coincidence of wants becomes dynamic and sustainable if confidence in the value of money condition is fulfilled.

The two-period OLG model is the simplest model and suitable for this line of thought.[5] The younger generation, which produces current goods, sells in exchange for money to prepare for their retirement. This apparently corresponds to saving behavior. On the other hand, the older generation purchases current goods with money carried over from the previous period. Since they do not concur with the young generation's decision, their expenditure is independent of the number of incomes created by the younger generation. Thus, a real independent expenditure is introduced without a capital accumulation decision.

Nevertheless, an additional consideration is necessary: movement of the current price level. If the current price level moves freely without theoretical constraint (note that this never corresponds to the *exogenous* price stickiness assumption such as for menu costs and price staggering that originates from Calvo [1983]), it can fall appreciably and raise the purchasing power of money until full employment is achieved.

However, Otaki (2015, ch. 2) found that there is an endogenous constraint concerning the law of motion of equilibrium price sequences that is genetically independent of the nominal money supply. Rigorous discussion will be held in the next subsection. Here, I provide a heuristic line of thought.

A younger individual decides his participation decision by referring to the future price level because his living standard after retirement is vital. Accordingly, the nominal reservation wage depends not only on the current price level but also the future. A firm sets the current price in proportion to the nominal reservation wage (I assume that unemployment prevails and young workers behave as price takers) and hence the equilibrium current price level is an increasing function of the future price level that is unrelated to the nominal money supply. This logic indicates that the equilibrium price level sequence under rational expectations can be determined independently of the nominal money supply.

This may seem strange or erroneous to believers in the quantity theory of money. Nonetheless, this first-order difference equation describes our ordinary life. The current value of money (the inverse of the current price level) becomes positive because people rationally believe that money will continue to be precious in the future. In addition, almost all people do not consider the nominal money supply when they make economic decisions except during extraordinary situations (e.g., hyperinflation).

Therefore, the current price is kept invariant when the nominal money supply increases to the extent that confidence in the value of money is disrupted. In such a case, an expansionary fiscal-monetary policy, a part of real independent expenditure, creates new incomes and employment opportunities. To summarize, the following points are important:

i. Whether the second postulate should be abandoned is irrelevant to the construction of a theory of effective demand. This fact confirms that menu cost theory essentially belongs to a static traditional Keynesian approach.
ii. The real expenditure independent of the saving decision is crucial and the existing investment function theory does not contribute to capturing this concept.
iii. The real independent expenditure requires the introduction of the difficulty of the double coincidence of wants. In this sense, the theory of effective demand is peculiar to the monetary economy.

In the next section, I construct a basic model that implies a theory of effective demand.

2.6 THEORY OF EFFECTIVE DEMAND

This section reproduces Keynes's (1936) model as faithfully as possible. One thing should be mentioned: there is a difference between my discussion and *The General Theory* regarding the value about which people are confident. While the earlier discussion presumes that people are confident about the value of money, Keynes assumes that workers are confident about the value of labor in terms of money (i.e., nominal wage). The question about which of the two assumption is more plausible is moot. In this chapter, I submit to Keynes's assertion although I switch to the alternative in the remaining chapters.

Nevertheless, such a change in belief in the intrinsic value does not affect resource allocation achieved by the market mechanism. This is due to the fact that my model always contains one undetermined or predetermined variable. Money is a bubbly asset and cannot impose any endpoint to the extent that a monetary economy is sustainable. Thus, indeterminacy emerges as a phenomenon peculiar to a monetary economy.

2.6.1 The Model

Using the information provided by the previous subsection, I construct a two-period OLG model in stationary state.

2.6.1.1 Individuals

The lifetime utility function U is defined as

$$U \equiv u(c_1, c_2) - \delta_1 \cdot \beta, \tag{2.13}$$

where (c_1, c_2) is the lifetime consumption vector and β denotes the disutility of labor. $u(\cdot)$ is a linear homogenous utility function of lifetime consumption. δ_1 is a definition function that takes value unity when a younger individual participates and zero when he is unemployed. The net utility derived from working must be non-negative. Accordingly,

$$\frac{\bar{W}}{\psi(p_1, p_2)} - \beta \geq 0 \Leftrightarrow \frac{\bar{W}}{p_1} \geq \beta \cdot \psi\left(1, \frac{p_2}{p_1}\right) \tag{2.14}$$

should be held. The first term of the left-hand side of equation (2.14) is the indirect utility from lifetime consumption, where $\psi(\cdot)$ is a linear homogenous function and an increasing function of p_i. $\bar{W}$ denotes the intrinsic value of labor in terms of money that individuals rationally believe in. This is an extension of the second postulate of the classical school in the sense that equation (2.14) implies a dynamic incentive compatibility condition in labor supply.

When we assume a Cobb-Douglas utility function, $u \equiv [c_1]^{\alpha} \cdot [c_2]^{1-\alpha}, 0 < \alpha < 1$, to resume Keynes's argument, the younger generation's consumption becomes insensitive to a change in the inflation rate and is expressed as

$$c_1 = \alpha \cdot y. \tag{2.15}$$

2.6.1.2 The Government

I assume that the government finances its wasteful expenditure by issuing new money. Consequently, it must satisfy the following budget constraint:

$$p_1 g = M_1 - M_0 \Leftrightarrow g = \frac{M_1}{p_1} - \frac{M_0}{p_1}, \tag{2.16}$$

where g is the real government expenditure and (M_1, M_0) is the nominal supply of the current period and previous period, respectively.

2.6.1.3 Market Equilibrium: Theory of Effective Demand

Let the aggregate production function be defined as

$$y \equiv f(N), \tag{2.17}$$

where N denotes employment level. Curve AS in the first quadrant of figure 2.4 illustrates equation (2.17), where N^F corresponds to the full employment level.

Combining equations (2.15), (2.16), and (2.17), the aggregate demand is defined as

$$y^d \equiv \alpha \cdot f(N) + \frac{M_0}{p_1} + g = \alpha \cdot f(N) + m, m \equiv \frac{M_1}{p_1}, \tag{2.18}$$

where the second term on the right-hand side of equation (2.18) corresponds to the expenditure of the older generation. Because the law of motion of equilibrium price sequences designated by equation (2.14) is independent of the nominal supply, we can regard the real cash balance m as a policy variable. Curve AD corresponds to equation (2.18). The equilibrium of the goods market is achieved at intersection E, where the following holds:

$$y = y^d. \tag{2.19}$$

Keynes calls this equilibrium the aggregate output effective demand. The question is whether effective demand is compatible with supply-side incentives: profit maximization of a firm and net positive utility derived from labor supply.

The fourth quadrant of figure 2.4 depicts the equilibrium condition for the labor market. The maximization behavior of a firm implies that

$$f'(N) = \frac{\bar{W}}{p_1}. \tag{2.20}$$

Equation (2.20) is the downward labor demand curve $L^D L^D$ in figure 2.4. The incentive compatibility condition for the participation decision, which is defined by equation (2.14), is the lower area of horizontal curve $L^S L^S$. We must note that this curve shifts downward when rational disinflationary expectations prevail. This is because disinflation improves the rate of return for money, and hence individuals accept a reduction in the real wage. It is apparent from figure 2.4 that if the real cash balance m

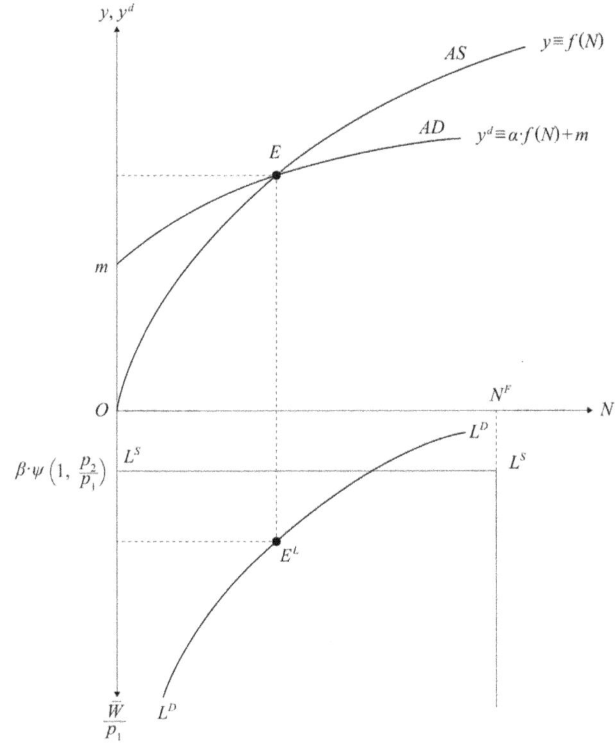

Figure 2.4 General equilibrium of OLG model. *Source*: Author.

is sufficiently small and the labor market is in equilibrium at point E^L, underemployment equilibrium exists. Furthermore, we must note that such unemployment is *involuntary* because E^L is located below curve $L^S L^S$.

Meanwhile, we can support Keynes's assertion that a reduction of the nominal wage $\bar{W}$ has no economic consequence other than a proportional reduction of the price level p_1. My model is built from equations (2.14), (2.17), (2.18), (2.19), and (2.20). The endogenous variables are $\left[y, y^d, N, \left(\bar{W}/p_1\right), \left(p_2/p_1\right)\right]$. Accordingly, as long as (p_1, p_2) decreases proportionately, there is no substantial change in such a rational expectations equilibrium, and hence Keynes's assertion is verified.

2.7 CONCLUDING REMARKS

In this chapter, I have analyzed a conundrum in monetary economics—the existence of idle production resources such as involuntary unemployment. Obtained results are as follows.

First, the second postulate of classical economics, which asserts that the real wage is no less than the corresponding disutility of labor, is unrelated to involuntary unemployment. When the independent expenditure of income is small, the associated production/employment reduces and hence heightens the marginal productivity of labor. This implies that the real wage offered by a firm possibly exceeds the disutility of labor and such a wage is compatible with workers' incentive. Accordingly, the second postulate does not hinder the description of involuntary unemployment. Meanwhile, I have shown that menu cost theory is a minor extension of traditional Keynesian theory that presumes some ad hoc exogenous price stickiness.

Second, while the labor-supply incentive is not essential in Keynesian economics, I found that the existence of the independent expenditure is crucial. However, we must note that the establishment of the investment function does not succeed in segregating aggregate demand from aggregate supply. This is because the incumbent investment function theory assumes that a firm plans capital investment to maximize its stock market value. To the extent that the stock price is determined rationally, it values the discounted sum of future dividends. In other words, capital investment amounts to surrogate savings of individuals. Therefore, aggregate saving is always equal to aggregate investment, and Say's law is still preserved.

Finally, the separation of aggregate demand from supply is achieved by introducing the difficulty of the double coincidence of wants. There are two existing methods to achieve the goal: the OLG model and search model. Nevertheless, the OLG model is far more operational than the latter. In the OLG model with money, whereas the older generation is interested only in the present, younger individuals are more concerned about their future. Thus, the older generation's money expenditure is autonomous and independent of the total income earned by the younger generation. As I have shown above, such an attempt succeeds in showing the existence of involuntary unemployment.

NOTES

1. For a precise discussion, see Keynes (1936, ch. 12).
2. Otaki (2016b) provides a tentative calculation of this discussion. Mathematically, separation of decisions is defined by the property that an economic agent's maximization problem cannot be represented by a part of the other economic agent's maximization problem.
3. This expression means that the employment and capital accumulation decision is decentralized (i.e., the representative individual does not account for the derivative effect that capital accumulation provides more employment opportunities). Meanwhile, in the case of concave instantaneous utility function, the stationary state

becomes undefinable, because the consumption increases at the same rate as capital accumulation.

4. Keynes (1936, ch. 12) emphasizes the divergence of the market value from the fundamental value. He argues that liquidation of capital investment possibly prompts volatile long-term expectations and seriously affects capital investment.

5. The search model, which originates in Diamond (1982) is an alternative idea. However, as Otaki (2015, ch. 15) shows, the search model is far less tractable than the OLG model.

Chapter 3

Origin of Speculative Bubbles and Their Aftermath

ABSTRACT

We define a speculative bubble as the phenomenon in which zero expected return assets possess positive economic values. The limited liability principle matters in such a case. Investors prefer higher risk and higher return assets under limited liability because they do not suffer serious damage when a bad state occurs. Accordingly, even the zero expected return assets have a positive market value.

However, a substantial amount of government subsidy should be introduced to the market to make the limited liability principle effective. As circulation of such assets implies the prevalence of an economy-wide zero-sum game, if we presume the limited liability principle, additional provision of an official subsidy becomes unavoidable. This finding implies that the precariousness of whether a speculative bubble emerges depends predominantly on the fiscal discipline of a government.

A huge amount of public debt might be accumulated with the government's aid to the financial market. I negate not only the Ricardian equivalence theorem under non-altruistic individuals but also Lerner's assertion that the issuance of public debt is irrelevant to future resource allocation. Therefore, speculative bubbles distort intergenerational resource allocation, and hence intergenerational ethics on macroeconomic policy should be established.

3.1. INTRODUCTION

This chapter, based on Otaki (2016a), considers one of the important causes of speculative bubbles, taking into account the events of the bubble boom from the late 1980s to the beginning of the 1990s in Japan. The most important characteristic of actual bubbles that differs from the prediction of the traditional theory originated in Blanchard and Watson (1982) is that the realized rate of return for bubbly assets far exceeds that for safe assets. In Japan, the realized rate of return for stocks and immobile assets during the bubble was recorded at 60 percent per annum. Traditional theory fails to explain this feverish phenomenon because such theory presumes that the interest arbitrage is always between that for bubbly assets and safe assets.

The moral hazard under limited liability plays a key role in explaining this seemingly irrational economic behavior. Even though the expected rate of return for a risky asset is zero, under a naïve limited liability in which the monetary authority and financial intermediaries do not have sufficient information on properties of the risky asset, the realized average rate of return becomes positive because investors become immune to the downside risk of such an asset.

The original aim of limited liability is to enhance investment in projects that are socially beneficial but are too risky. However, whenever financial intermediaries are incautious during project assessment and the monetary authority is excessively benevolent to failures in financial intermediaries (including unlimited allowance for bailout), as the *Guarded Convoy Method* discussed the case of Japan in chapter 1, limited liability malfunctions and provokes morally hazardous behavior. Even an asset with an original expected return of zero comes to possess a positive value under limited liability. Worse still, higher-risk and higher-return assets are preferred because investors are permitted to positively skew their returns under such a risky limited liability system.

The most prominent aim of this chapter is to pursue the macroeconomic consequences of failures in massive speculative investments that are prompted by incompetence of financial intermediaries and the monetary authority. We must note that there is no private agent who undertakes deficits emerging from such misconduct. Ultimately, the monetary authority is obliged to purchase these non-performing debts. This assertion is facile to be ascertained when we consider the accounting of the overall economy.

This hard fact implies that consecutive and huge fiscal deficits are unavoidable and trigger a rapid accumulation of public debt as observed in the Japanese economy during the 1990s. Whether the redemption of public debt becomes a burden on future generations is vital because it is hard to imagine that such a large amount of public debt can be redeemed within the same generation as it is issued.

Barro (1974) assumes an altruistic individual whose utility function contains the same alternatives of his descendants and suggests that the current issue of public debt is recognized exactly as a future tax liability. This is because such an individual takes into consideration budget constraints of future generations. Nevertheless, this is an excessively restrictive assumption. In addition, if his thesis is legitimate, speculative bubbles that decisively rely on the rescue scheme accompanying new issuance of public debt are never provoked because people correctly perceive the future tax liability. Therefore, it is natural to regard economic decisions as being demarcated generation by generation.

Lerner (1944) asserts that the redemption of public debt does not impose any burden on future generations because such redemption merely alters the income distribution within the same generation. If Lerner's assertion is valid, there are no substantial changes in resource allocation by the market mechanism.

This chapter shows that Lerner's assertion is invalid and that the redemption of public debt carried over from the ascendants aggravates the economic welfare of the generation in charge of the redemption. The scenario is simple and an application of the multiplier theory. We must note that the marginal propensity of the older generation to consume is unity, and thus, the redemption of public debt compensating for non-performing private debt reduces the nominal money supply to the level of the pre-bubble period. On the other hand, the same amount of tax is deducted from the younger generation's income. Accordingly, such redemption can be regarded as additional income taxation with a multiplier that is the inverse of the marginal propensity to save.

We must note that a decrease in real disposable income coincidently aggravates the economic welfare of the younger generation in charge of the redemption. To summarize, against Lerner's intuition, the redemption of public debt becomes a burden on future generations. In this sense, speculative bubbles are undesirable from the point of view of intergenerational ethics.

The rest of the chapter is organized as follows. Section 3.2 provides an overlapping-generations (OLG) model that contains a bubbly asset. In section 3.3, a comparative statics is conducted, revealing that a soft-budget government tends to cause speculative bubbles. Section 3.4 contains brief concluding remarks.

3.2. THE MODEL

Before constructing the model, I show modifications from the model in chapter 2.

1. Monopolistic Competition: Chapter 2 assumes perfect competition. Instead, this chapter uses monopolistic competition as the equilibrium

concept of the goods market. This assumption implies that monopoly rent emerges in the model. However, we must note such rent contributes to economic welfare through an increase in dividends, which individuals equally receive. Since I assume that the production function is a linear function of labor, surplus evaporates in the case of perfect competition. Furthermore, we must note that a social shortage of supply of employment and output owing to monopolistic behavior never emerges in the model as in the new Keynesian model. This is because I establish that the aggregate demand is defined independently of the aggregate supply. This property implies that imperfect employment is caused by the shortage of aggregate demand and not by the monopolistic behavior of firms. We must note that resource allocation in the equilibrium state of new Keynesian model, which is static by nature, becomes second best indicator of a failure of the model in constructing the notion of effective demand that is definable in a dynamic situation. This was discussed at length in chapter 2.

2. CES Instantaneous Utility Function: As discussed in chapter 2, a rational price index is obtainable only when an instantaneous utility function is linear and homogenous. A constant elasticity of substitution (CES) function satisfies this requirement. Meanwhile, I would like to exclude the non-linearity in output price setting. Thus, the price elasticity of each good should be invariant along with a change in the demand. Consequently, a CES function should be deployed.

3.2.1 Individuals

Based on the models developed by Otaki (2007, 2015, 2016a), a two-period OLG model with a bubbly asset has been constructed. The utility function of individual i, U_i, is

$$U_i \equiv u\left(c_{it}, c_{it+1}\right) - \delta_{it} \cdot \beta, c_{it} \equiv \left[\sum_{j=1}^{m} \left[c_{it}(j)\right]^{1-\eta^{-1}}\right]^{\frac{1}{1-\eta^{-1}}}, 1 < \eta, \tag{3.1}$$

where u is a linear homogenous and strictly concave function that represents the utility obtained by lifetime consumption. β denotes the disutility of labor. δ_{it} is a definition function that takes the unity when the individual is employed and zero when unemployed. There are a large number of individuals, n, which upholds the law of large numbers.

The labor market equilibrium is assumed to be interior in the sense that some individuals are always unemployed in equilibrium. There are m kinds of goods. For simplicity, marginal labor productivity is assumed to be unity in the overall economy and a commodity is monopolistically produced by the corresponding firm.

Fiat money is the only transaction and value hoarding medium. However, money in this context means widely defined liquidity, which includes public debt. As the world economy is currently facing a historical low interest era, we neglect the interest payment for public debt.

In addition to the widely defined liquidity, ahead of all other economic decisions, there is an investment opportunity for risky assets whose expected net return is zero. Let the return on this asset be denoted by x_θ. The ex-post rate of return on this asset, ξ_θ, is written as

$$\xi_\theta \equiv \max\left[x_\theta, 0\right], \tag{3.2}$$

under the limited liability principle. θ denotes the risk class of this kind of asset. The risk is classified according to the criterion of second-order stochastic dominance (mean preserving spread). That is, if and only if asset θ_1 is riskier than asset θ_2, then the equation

$$\int_{-\underline{x}}^{x} F_{\theta_1}\left(x_{\theta_1}\right) dx_{\theta_1} \geq \int_{-\underline{x}}^{x} F_{\theta_2}\left(x_{\theta_2}\right) dx_{\theta_2}, \forall x \leq \overline{x} \tag{3.3}$$

holds. $F_\theta(x_\theta)$ denotes the cumulative distribution function (CDF) of x_θ. Equality holds only when $x = \overline{x}$. The interval $\left[\underline{x}, \overline{x}\right]$ is the domain of x_θ. It is assumed that the expected return without the limited liability principle is zero. This leads us to the following equation:[1]

$$\overline{x} - \int_{\underline{x}}^{\overline{x}} F\left(x_\theta\right) dx_\theta = 0, \forall \theta. \tag{3.4}$$

In addition, an elementary calculus leads us to

$$E\left[\xi_{\theta_1}\right] > E\left[\xi_{\theta_2}\right]. \tag{3.5}$$

This is the property that Stiglitz and Weiss (1981) induce.

An elementary example of the second-order stochastic is as follows: assume that there are two states 1 (bad state) and 2 (good state) which-possibly occur 1/2 each. In addition, each expected return is zero. Asset A is a low-risk asset with return profile of $(-x_A, x_A)$. Asset B is a high-risk asset with return profile of $(-x_B, x_B)$, where $(0 < x_A < x_B)$. Under the limited-liability principle of equation (3.2), each expected return becomes

$$E(\xi_A) = \frac{x_A}{2}, E(\xi_B) = \frac{x_B}{2} \Rightarrow E(\xi_B) > E(\xi_A). \tag{3.6}$$

Thus, the riskier asset is preferred under the limited-liability principle. The lifetime budget constraint after the revelation of the value of $x_{i\theta t}$ becomes

$$p_t c_{it} + p_{t+1} c_{it+1} \le w_{it}\delta_{it} + \pi_{it} + p_t \xi_{i\theta t} - p_t \tau_{it}, p_t \equiv \left[\sum_{j=1}^{m} \left[\frac{p_t(j)}{m} \right]^{1-\eta} \right]^{\frac{1}{1-\eta}}, \tag{3.7}$$

where π_{it} refers to the nominal profits that individual i receives.

The corresponding indirect utility function I_{it} is

$$I_{it} \equiv \frac{w_{it}\delta_{it} + \pi_{it} + p_t \xi_{i\theta t}}{\Psi(p_t, p_{t+1})} - \delta_{it}\beta, \tag{3.8}$$

where Ψ is a linear homogenous function. Since it is assumed that the equilibrium of the labor market is interior in the sense that some individuals are always unemployed, the equilibrium condition requires that there is no gain by being employed. Accordingly, from equation (3.8), the equilibrium nominal wage becomes

$$w_t = \beta \cdot \Psi(p_t, p_{t+1}). \tag{3.9}$$

Meanwhile, since the indirect utility function is a linear function of $\xi_{i\theta t}$, the choice of bubbly asset is separable from other economic decisions; hence, all individuals invest in the riskiest bubbly asset as far as admissible. This is apparent from inequality (3.5). If an economy consists of innumerable individuals and the law of large numbers is upheld, the average private return from such an asset is $\overline{x} - \int_0^{\overline{x}} F(x_{\overline{\theta}}) dx_{\overline{\theta}}$, where $\overline{\theta}$ denotes the admissibly riskier asset. Whenever $\overline{\theta}$ is risky enough, from inequality (3.5), one must note that the average rate of return of the bubbly asset exceeds that of the alternative investment avenue: money.

From equation (3.4), the following relationship is obtained:

$$\overline{x} - \int_0^{\overline{x}} F(x_{\overline{\theta}}) dx_{\overline{\theta}} = \int_{\underline{x}}^{0} F(x_{\overline{\theta}}) dx_{\overline{\theta}}. \tag{3.10}$$

The right-hand side of equation (3.10) represents the aggregate capital loss of the overall economy. This is a natural consequence that comes from the fact that speculating a bubbly asset is essentially equal to participating in a zero-sum game.

What is important in this vein is that a subsidy from the government is necessary to sustain the limited liability principle. As evident in equation (3.10), a substantial number of individuals lose money beyond their payment ability. Therefore, once the capital gains of certain investors are actualized, the government has to incur the cost of the subsidy to compensate the capital loss even though in reality considerable time elapses before compensation is made. Purchasing non-performing debts that emerged from the speculative bubble is a typical example. It is assumed that such expenditure is entirely financed by the issuance of new money.

Lastly, as the lifetime utility function is assumed to be linear homogenous, one obtains the following aggregate consumption function, c, of the young individual:

$$c \equiv c(\rho)y_t, y_t \equiv \frac{Y_t}{p_r}, \rho \equiv \frac{p_{t+1}}{p_t}, c' > 0, 0 < c(\cdot) < 1, \tag{3.11}$$

where Y_t and y_t are nominal and real aggregate incomes.

3.2.2 Firms

Firm j faces the following demand function, D_j:

$$D_{jt} \equiv \left[\frac{p_t(j)}{p_t}\right]^{-\eta} \cdot y_{jt}, y_{jt} \equiv \frac{Y_t}{mp_t}, \tag{3.12}$$

where y_{it} is the real aggregate income per firm. Accordingly, the profit-maximization condition leads us to

$$p_t(j) = \frac{W_t}{1-\eta^{-1}}. \tag{3.13}$$

Substituting equation (3.9) into equation (3.13) and aggregating both sides of equation (3.12) on j, I obtain

$$p_t = \frac{\beta \cdot \Psi(p_t, p_{t+1})}{1-\eta^{-1}} \Leftrightarrow \Psi(1, \rho) = \frac{1-\eta^{-1}}{\beta}. \tag{3.14}$$

Equation (3.14) is vital for the theory. The equilibrium inflation rate (or the inverse of the rate of return of the widely defined liquidity) is determined by equation (3.14) unrelated to the nominal stock of the widely defined liquidity. This implies that an equilibrium path of price level can be unaffected by the monetary condition in an economy. Thus, liquidity becomes non-neutral even though there is no stickiness in prices and the nominal wage. Equation (3.14) enables us to analyze the macroeconomic implication of speculative bubbles.

3.2.3 The Government

The budget constraint of the government is denoted as

$$\tau_t + \frac{L_t - L_{t-1}}{p_t} = g + \chi_t \cdot \sum_{i=1}^{n} \xi_{\bar{\theta} it}, \tag{3.15}$$

where L_t is the supply of the widely defined liquidity. The left-hand side is the total revenue of the government, which consists of the real tax revenue τ_t and the real issuance of the new widely defined liquidity $(L_t - L_{t-1})/p_t$. The right-hand side is the real government expenditure toward the infrastructure that is indispensable to sustain the economy. It is assumed that government expenditure for each commodity will follow the same pattern as that of the individual. χ_t is a definition function that takes value unity when speculative bubbles are provoked and zero when bubbles are suppressed by prudent monetary policy. The second term of the right-hand side of equation (3.15) denotes the sum of the compensation for non-performing assets whose returns are negative. By deploying the law of large numbers, equation (3.15) can be rewritten as

$$l_{nt} - \frac{l_{nt-1}}{\rho} = \left[g_{nt} - \tau_{nt}\right] + \chi_t \cdot E\left(\xi_{\bar{\theta} t}\right), \tag{3.16}$$

where subscript n means that the variables are measured in per capita terms. Equation (3.16) implies that the additional widely defined liquidity per capita is entirely included in the compensation for the burst bubble at period t and redeemed within the subsequent period. To put it differently, whenever individuals rationally expect the monetary authority to adopt a more forbearing policy, they speculate a riskier zero-sum asset (they choose an asset that takes a higher value of $\bar{\theta}$).

3.2.4 Market Equilibrium

There are three markets in this model: the goods market, the liquidity market, and the labor market. The two former markets are not independent from the budget constraints of the young generation (3.6) and the government's budget constraint (3.16). The aggregate goods market achieves the equilibrium when

$$\begin{aligned} y_{nt} &= c(\rho)\left[y_{nt} - \tau_{nt} + \chi_t \cdot E(\xi_{\bar{\theta}})\right] + g_n + \chi_t \cdot E(\xi_{\bar{\theta}}) + \frac{l_{nt-1}}{\rho} \\ \Leftrightarrow y_{nt} &= c(\rho)\left[y_{nt} - \tau_{nt} + \chi_t \cdot E(\xi_{\bar{\theta}})\right] + \tau_{nt} + l_{nt}, l_{nt} \equiv \frac{L_{nt}}{p_t}. \end{aligned} \tag{3.17}$$

Policy variables are the real tax per capita, τ_{nt}, and the real liquidity per capita, l_{nt}. The endogenous variables are the real income per capita, y_{nt} and the inflation rate, ρ. The structural equations are equations (3.14) and (3.17). Thus, the model is completely closed.

3.3. COMPARATIVE STATICS

3.3.1 Monetary-Fiscal Policy and Speculative Bubbles

This subsection deals with how the tightness of monetary-fiscal policy affects the seriousness of the consequence of speculative bubbles. Differentiating both sides of equation (3.17), the following result is obtained:

$$\frac{dy_{nt}}{d\bar{\theta}} = \frac{1}{1 - c(\rho)}\left[1 + c(\rho)\right]\frac{dE(\xi_{\bar{\theta}})}{d\bar{\theta}}. \tag{3.18}$$

Equation (3.18) implies that emerge two expansionary effects emerge through adoption of a compromising policy by the monetary authority: one is the direct effect that increases disposable income by raising the average rate of return for the bubbly asset. This effect appears in the second term inside the bracket in equation (3.18), the magnitude of which is equal to the value of the multiplier of tax reduction, $c(\rho)/[1 - c(\rho)]$. The other is the indirect effect, which comes from the expansion of the widely defined liquidity provided for compensation for the busted bubble. The magnitude of this effect is the pure multiplier, $1/[1 - c(\rho)]$, as is evident from the first term in the bracket of equation (3.18).

Thus, while the debt incurred by the bursting of the bubble piles up in conjunction with the compromised and accommodative monetary policy, such a policy possesses an explosive power to upturn business. This ephemeral temptation urges people to boost the bubble, which results in leaving the burden for the future generation as discussed in the next subsection.

3.3.2 Speculative Bubbles as a Burden for the Future Generation

This subsection considers the intergenerational economic consequence of speculative bubbles. It is assumed that the bubble inflates and bursts during period t and the economic welfare is compared with that during the aftermath of the bubble (the welfare of generation t+1). As a reference point, let the welfare of the pre-bubble generation t–1 be calculated as well.

For simplicity, it is assumed that $\tau_{t-i} = 0, \forall i \geq 0$. From equation (3.17), the equilibrium income per capita of generation t–1, y_{nt-1} becomes

$$y_{nt-1} = \frac{l_n}{1-c(\rho)}, l_n \equiv \frac{g}{1-\frac{1}{\rho}}. \tag{3.19}$$

Similarly, y_{nt}, y_{nt+1} becomes

$$\begin{aligned} y_{nt} &= \frac{l_n + \left[1+c(\rho)\right]E(\xi_{\bar{\theta}})}{1-c(\rho)}, \\ y_{nt+1} - \tau_{nt+1} &= \frac{l_n - \tau_{nt+1}}{1-c(\rho)}, \tau_{nt+1} = \frac{E(\xi_{\bar{\theta}})}{\rho}. \end{aligned} \tag{3.20}$$

As illustrated in figure 3.1, the rational speculative bubble triggered by a lax monetary policy boosts an economy ephemerally. When the government decides to redeem non-performing debts, which amount to $\left[E(\xi_{\bar{\theta}})\right]/\rho$, the young generation after the bubble period suffers from the bursting of the bubble, and hence, according to equations (3.19) and (3.20), their disposable real income decreases by $\left[1/1-c(\rho)\right] \cdot \left[E(\xi_{\bar{\theta}})/\rho\right]$. This is an elementary application of the fiscal multiplier theory.

Equations (3.19) and (3.20) reflect the fact that there is a serious burden on the future generation, that stems from the speculative bubble in the current period. Using the indirect utility function (3.7), the equilibrium utility of an individual who belongs to generation t+i is rewritten as

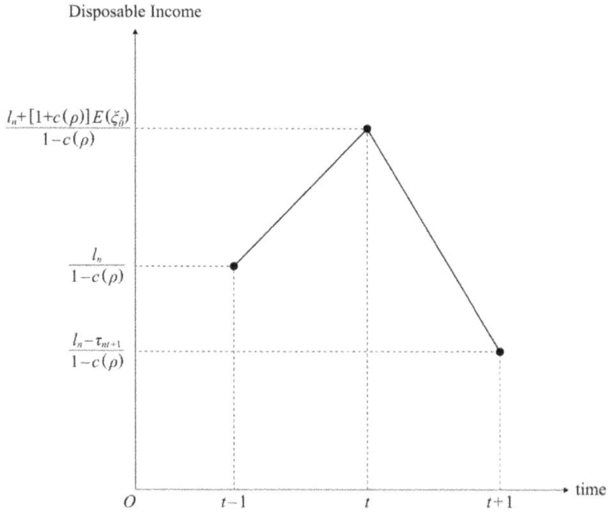

Figure 3.1 Speculative bubbles and disposable income. *Source*: Author.

$$IU_{t+i} = \frac{\eta^{-1} y_{nt+i} - \tau_{nt+i}}{\Psi(1,\rho)}, \tag{3.21}$$

where $\eta^{-1}y_{nt+i}$ is the income accrued from profits (note that there is no welfare gain from working because the nominal wage stacks at the nominal reservation wage in the imperfect employment equilibrium).

A speculative bubble becomes a burden on the future generation in the sense that the individual's well-being is lowered compared with those in the pre-bubble generation t–1. Equation (3.21) can be transformed as

$$\begin{aligned} IU_{t+1} &= \frac{\eta^{-1} y_{nt+1} - \tau_{nt+1}}{\Psi(1,\rho)} \\ &= \frac{\eta^{-1}\left[y_{nt+1} - \tau_{nt+1}\right] - \left[1-\eta^{-1}\right]\tau_{nt+1}}{\Psi(1,\rho)} < \frac{\eta^{-1} y_{nt-1}}{\Psi(1,\rho)} \\ &= IU_{t-1}. \end{aligned} \tag{3.22}$$

In this sense, Lerner's assertion (1944) is incorrect even in a Keynesian framework that allows the possibility of imperfect unemployment equilibrium. Even though the supply of widely defined liquidity remains unchanged between the pre-bubble and post-bubble generations, the bubble generation (generation t) imposes on the post-bubble generation the burden of redeeming the excess widely defined liquidity. We must note that substantial amounts of income are transferred via the government from the younger generation to the older generation who enjoyed the bubble, and this aggravates the economic welfare of the young generation. Meanwhile, such a burden is heavier when the monetary policy is laxer and the current generation anticipates that it is permitted to invest in riskier assets. This statement is ascertained by equation (3.20).

3.3.3 Precariousness of Repeated Bubbles: The Importance of Intergenerational Ethics

As discussed in the previous subsection, redemption of the liquidity issued for offsetting the loss of the bubbly asset lowers the welfare of the subsequent generation eventually. Moreover, a speculative bubble brings ephemeral prosperity to the current generation. Accordingly, the monetary authority dislikes redemption and prefers to cause a speculative bubble once again. As such, once a compromised monetary policy is settled, speculative bubbles are caused successively. This implies that a huge amount of widely defined liquidity is injected into an economy incessantly.

One must note that there is an upper limit in the volume of circulating liquidity beyond which public confidence about its value as a measure of goods wanes. Let us assume that the economy reaches the critical point by successive bubbles, in which people start to hold rational expectations in line with the quantity theory of money. Such expectations imply that people disbelieve the intrinsic value of money even though they continue using money.[2] Let the equilibrium price function be denoted as

$$p_t = \kappa L_t. \tag{3.23}$$

It is shown that an additional issue of widely defined liquidity entirely crowds out the consumption opportunities of the older generation. The proof is elementary. Rewriting equation (3.16) with consideration of equation (3.23), we obtain

$$\kappa^{-1} = g + \frac{\kappa^{-1}}{\mu}. \tag{3.24}$$

The first term on the right-hand side of equation (3.24) is real government expenditure, and the second term denotes real consumption of the older generation. It is apparent that the growth rate of widely defined liquidity μ should be increased and the revenue of inflation tax accrued from nominal asset holders (older individuals) finances the increment in government expenditure. It is also evident from equation (3.24) that such a crowding-out effect is perfect when disbelief in the intrinsic value of money and the quantity-theoretic rational expectations prevail.

We should note that the discussion above implies that the aggregate-demand management policy is hindered by the prevalence of disbelief in the value of money. Indeed, the policy is detrimental because scarce consumption opportunities after retirement are lost through wasteful government expenditure via increases in inflation tax.

Therefore, the government will lose the ability to stabilize the economy because of disbelief in the intrinsic value of money that is a devastating consequence of repeated speculative bubbles and implies the bursting of the bubble of money itself. Since the constant κ in equation (3.23) can take an arbitrarily positive value, and it is plausible to consider that κ takes quite a large value when such disbelief is viral, the economy will experience a severe stagnation arising from the shortage of the purchasing power of money. We must note that the neutrality of money does not necessarily imply the achievement of full-employment equilibrium.

3.4 CONCLUDING REMARKS

This chapter explored the origin of speculative bubbles and analyzed the economic consequences. The obtained results are as follows. First, a feverish bubble, with a rate of return exceeding the rate of interest, originates from the limited liability principle under asymmetric information. In other words, a feverish bubble is a kind of moral hazard that is implicit in the government's pecuniary compensation for defeated investors.

Second, a feverish bubble improves the welfare of the concurrent generation. This is partly because a higher rate of return of the bubbly asset increases aggregate disposable income, and partly because the newly issued liquidity injected for the compensation of defeated investors creates additional aggregate demand via the multiplier process. However, whenever the additional liquidity is redeemed by the subsequent generation, this becomes a burden for the descendants in the sense that their well-being is lower compared with those in the pre-bubble generation. Thus, a myopic government is eager to avoid the redemption and prefers to continue the feverish bubble.

Lastly, when widely defined liquidity accumulates into a huge amount through incessant bubbles, individuals start to disbelieve the intrinsic value of money, and as a result, the quantity theoretic rational expectation prevails. When such an expectation is created, the government is unable to control the economy. This is because people regard the purchasing power of money as invariant, and an expansionary fiscal policy completely crowds out older individuals' consumption. This would exhaust the resources of the government unless it resumes sufficient levying ability instead of inflation tax, which endangers the supply of infrastructure, the foundation of the economy.

NOTES

1. For further detail on equations (3.4) and (3.5), see appendix C.
2. To preserve the incentive compatibility condition of labor supply, the increased rate of widely defined liquidity, $\mu \equiv (l_{t+1})/lt$, should satisfy the following inequality that is derived from equation (3.14):

$$p_t \geq \frac{\beta \cdot \Psi(p_t, p_{t+1})}{1-\eta^{-1}} \Leftrightarrow \Psi(1,\mu) \leq \frac{1-\eta^{-1}}{\beta}.$$

Let $\kappa_0^{-1} \equiv \left(\frac{l_{n0}}{p_0}\right)$ be denoted as the initial position before the quantity theoretic expectation prevails. Since the quantity theory of money is a rational belief, which regards that there is a fixed parity between goods and liquidity, κ_0^{-1} might be far larger than κ^{-1} when disbelief in the intrinsic value of money begins to prevail. Accordingly, once such an expectation is generated, the current price level jumps drastically in the following way: individuals anticipate the jump of the price level, and thus they try to purchase goods in exchange of money. However, since all individuals take the same action, the rise of the price level or the depreciation of the nominal value of the widely defined liquidity (i.e., the price of public debt) makes κ_0^{-1} lower than κ^{-1}. To put it succinctly, when disbelief in the intrinsic value of money is distilled under the excess liquidity situation, hyperinflation and/or a plummet of the price of public debt ensues.

Chapter 4

Labor Productivity Stagnation, the Radical Quantitative Easing of Monetary Policy, and Disinflation

ABSTRACT

There is an anomaly observed in many advanced economies—disinflation accompanied by stagnation of labor productivity. In a static barter economy, this phenomenon is incomprehensible because labor productivity stagnation relative to aggregate demand raises price levels. That is, theoretically, disinflation can coexist only with the rapid progress of labor productivity. I construct an overlapping-generations model (OLG model), which predicts disinflation caused by a slowdown in labor productivity. The crucial factor is that demand for current goods can decrease when labor productivity slows down. This implies that disinflation and recession coexist to keep equilibrium in the goods market. In addition, I clarify the reason why quantitative easing (QE) policy such as that seen in Japan and other advanced economies causes mild disinflation.

4.1 INTRODUCTION

This chapter develops a theory to explain worldwide disinflation around the turn of the century that is an application of the basic model in chapter 2.

As suggested in table 4.1, disinflation and the slowdown of labor productivity growth is prominent in advanced countries. Beyond the issue of measurement errors,[1] these phenomena are related to different factors. For example, according to ECB (2016), labor productivity slowdown in the US is mainly attributed to

i. Decrease in capital deepening, and
ii. Slowdown of total factor productivity (TFP) growth.

Table 4.1 Labor Productivity Progress and Inflation Rate

Year	*Labor Productivity Progress (%)*	*Inflation Rate (%)*
2001	1.7	3.6
2002	1.7	2.7
2003	2.3	2.4
2004	2.2	2.6
2005	1.6	2.6
2006	1.5	2.5
2007	1.4	3.6
2008	–0.1	0.51
2009	0.3	1.8
2010	1.8	2.9
2011	1.3	2.2
2012	0.3	1.6
2013	1.1	1.7
2014	0.6	0.6
2015	0.9	1.1

Data Source: OECD Employment and Market Statistics.

On the other hand, as a key variable of disinflation, inflation expectations are frequently examined although their findings span a wide range. Christensen (2009) revealed that minor investors held deflationary expectations even during the deflation era in the US Piazza (2015) found that Japanese deflationary expectations are prominent compared with the world economy. Hori and Shimizutani (2005) showed that Japanese inflation expectations are strongly affected by their own lagged variables.

However, the slowdown of capital deepening or TFP is not consistent with disinflation in the classical static model, regardless of what price expectations may be. For example, let us consider a classical two-production factor linear homogenous production function model, which the TFP analysis implicitly assumes. If capital deepening decelerates, labor becomes the abundant resource. Accordingly, the real wage becomes lower relative to the real rent. Nevertheless, this model does not possess the power to determine price levels because it is a classical real model, which cannot introduce money endogenously. Hence, by definition, it is impossible to know whether disinflation occurs or not.

Instead, consider the case in which capital accumulation takes time to be effective, and capital is a quasi-fixed factor in the short run. Hence, labor is the only variable production resource. In such a case, if the nominal wage is fixed, the price level potentially increases. This is because the upward-sloping aggregate supply curve shifts leftward against the upward-sloping aggregate demand curve. It is not disinflation but *static* inflation. It must be noted that this scenario, which is based on standard Keynesian theory, is a variant of the stagflation model of Bruno and Sachs (1985), and thus neither the neoclassical nor Keynesian type models can explain the coexistence of disinflation and labor productivity slowdown since the model is basically *static*.

Therefore, we must note that disinflation is a dynamic phenomenon in a monetary economy. The current and future economy is linked through money. In addition, output price is measured in terms of money. Accordingly, we need a dynamic model with money to analyze the coexistence of disinflation and productivity slowdown.

The two period overlapping-generations (OLG) model with money is the simplest and most suitable analytical tool. Chapter 2 develops such a model based on Otaki (2007, 2009, 2015); this type of OLG model has the property that the value of money (the inverse of the price index) is determined by the rational expectation of its own future value, and thus unemployment emerges whenever the real cash balance is sufficiently small with no rigidity assumption on prices. I assume a linear production function of labor with exogenously given labor productivity to facilitate the comparative statics.

An exogenous labor productivity slowdown implies that the current potential aggregated supply is curtailed. Since young individuals' consumption is an increasing function of the *ex-ante* inflation rate, which is equal to the *ex-post* inflation of the next period under rational expectations equilibrium (REE), disinflation is provoked to equilibrate the current goods market. Thus, in a monetary economy, disinflation can coexist with a productivity slowdown.

It is important to distinguish between *ex-post* and *ex-ante* inflation. Let t be the current period. Then, the *ex-post* inflation, π^{EP}, is defined as

$$\pi^{EP} \equiv \frac{p_t}{p_{t-1}}. \tag{4.1}$$

The *ex-ante* rational expectation, π^{EX}, which affects young individuals' decisions, is

$$\pi^{EX} \equiv \frac{p_{t+1}}{p_t}. \tag{4.2}$$

As discussed above, the *ex-post* inflation rate can be derived from the comparative statics of a neoclassical model. However, the *ex-ante* inflation rate, which is equal to the future actual inflation rate (*ex-post* inflation rate during period t+1 under REE), can only be derived in a dynamic model. It must be noted that what is important for determining the equilibrium is the *ex-ante* inflation rate, and not the *ex-post* inflation rate, because those who substantially determine the resource allocation of the overall economy are the current young generation. The classical static model cannot derive the *ex-ante* inflation rate by definition. The strict distinction between the price level and inflation rate is crucial for macroeconomic theory.

Regarding the origins of deflation, my model is also useful in analyzing the consequences of the radical quantitative easing (QE) monetary policy. Disinflation continues in advanced economies despite the intention of the radical QE policy. This is paradoxical for those who follow quantity theory including new Keynesians.[2] In contrast, my model can explain this phenomenon.

The OLG model assumes that individuals are *confident* of the intrinsic value of money in the sense that they rationally believe the current price level is independent of the nominal money supply. An increase in the nominal money supply requires deflation. This is because the aggregate savings of the young generation should increase to equilibrate the money market.

The most prominent future of the OLG model is that a change in some stock macroeconomic variable such as the nominal money supply can *directly* affect flow variables. Traditional IS/LM analysis (including sophisticated versions of new Keynesian) cannot analyze how the new monetary inflow affects the equilibrium condition of the goods market. If a change in the stock variable is negligibly small, the IS/LM method can be considered a reasonable first-order approximation. However, the volume of the radical QE policy per annum is huge, and thus the OLG model is far more suitable than the IS/LM analysis to investigate its effects on the overall economy.

This chapter is organized as follows. Section 4.2 constructs a classical static model and a dynamic OLG model to exhibit different insights into the coexistence of disinflation and labor productivity slowdown. In section 4.3, I critically analyze effects of the radical QE policy by using the OLG model constructed in section 4.2. Section 4.4 contains concluding remarks.

4.2 THE MODEL

4.2.1 The Classical Real Model

I consider an economy in which one good is produced by one production resource: labor. The utility function, U, of the representative individual is assumed to be

$$U \equiv x - G(h), G' > 0, G'' > 0, \lim_{h \to 0} G'(h) = 0, \lim_{h \to +\infty} G'(h) = +\infty, \quad (4.3)$$

where x denotes the volume of consumption and h is the hours worked. The $G(\cdot)$ function represents the disutility from labor. The budget constraint is

$$Wh \geq px \Leftrightarrow \frac{W}{p}h \geq x, \tag{4.4}$$

where W denotes the nominal wage and p is the price of goods.

From the Inada condition in equation (4.3), the budget constraint, equation (4.4), is always binding. Therefore, the maximization problem, which the representative individual solves, is

$$\max_{h}\left[\frac{W}{p}h - G(h)\right] \Leftrightarrow \frac{W}{p} = G'(h). \tag{4.5}$$

Production is assumed to be linear on hours worked:

$$x = \gamma h. \tag{4.6}$$

Goods and labor markets are under perfect competition. Substituting equation (4.6), the zero-profit condition implies

$$\pi \equiv px - Wh = 0 \Leftrightarrow \frac{W}{p} = \gamma. \tag{4.7}$$

Accordingly, labor productivity is equalized to the real wage. The equilibrium of the goods market is illustrated by point E in figure 4.1. It is evident from figure 4.1 that optimal hours worked, h^*, is an increasing function of labor productivity γ. That is,

$$h^* = \varphi(\gamma),\ \varphi' > 0. \tag{4.8}$$

Here we assume that nominal wage, W, is the numeraire. Then we can determine the price of goods in terms of the nominal wage. Let this variable be denoted p_w. Since labor productivity is equal to the real wage (see equation [4.7]), the price, p_w, always increases when labor productivity slows down. Thus, *ex-post* inflation as represented in equation (4.1) is triggered by such a slowdown.

Furthermore, the curtailed real wage decreases the equilibrium hours worked, h^*. This implies that stagflation occurs in this economy. It should be noted that this property of the static neoclassical model is quite robust as shown in Bruno and Sachs (1985).

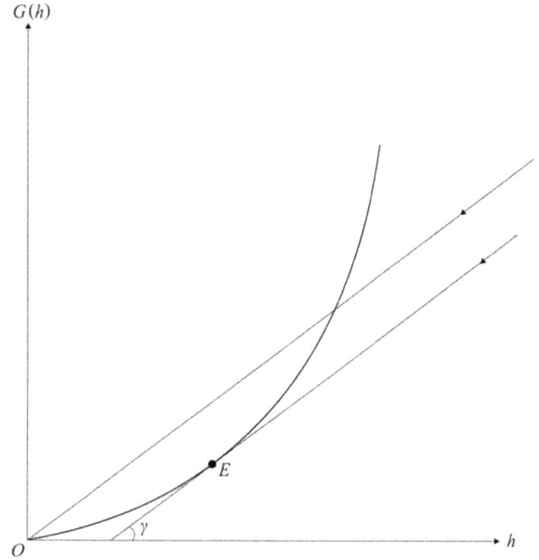

Figure 4.1 The static case. *Source*: Author.

Figure 4.2 illustrates the equilibrium of the goods market from another point of view. Horizontal line *SS* is the supply curve as defined in equation (4.7).[3] The downward-sloping curve *DD* is the demand curve of goods. This curve

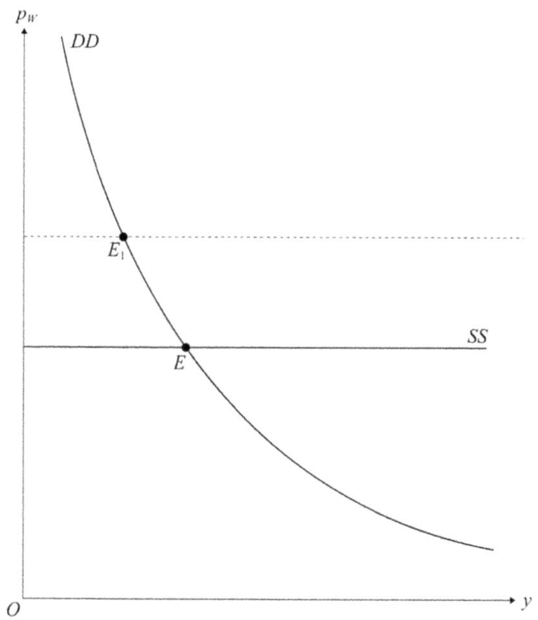

Figure 4.2 Neoclassical equilibrium. *Source*: Author.

can be derived in the following way. First, the optimal hours worked h^* is a decreasing function of the goods price p_w. Second, from the budget constraint equation (4.4), it is evident that the optimal consumption, x^*, increases in conjunction with h^*. Consequently, x^* is a decreasing function of p_w, and hence the demand curve *DD* becomes downward sloping. The equilibrium is achieved at point *E*.

It is also straightforward from figure 4.2 that the equilibrium moves toward the northwest point of *DD* such as point E_1 whenever labor productivity slowdown is provoked as a consequence of the upward shift of supply curve *SS*. This is the essence of the supply-shock model developed by Bruno and Sachs (1985).

To summarize, the real static model cannot explain the coexistence of disinflation and labor productivity slowdown. This fact suggests that a dynamic model with money is needed to solve this paradox.

4.2.2 The Two-Period Overlapping-Generations Model

I construct a two period OLG model with money and infinite time horizon in a production economy, which is developed by Lucas (1972) and Otaki (2007, 2009, 2015). The utility function, *V*, of a representative individual who is born at the beginning period *t* is

$$V \equiv v\left(x_{1t}, x_{2t+1}\right) - G\left(h_t\right), \tag{4.9}$$

where $v(\cdot)$ represents the utility from lifetime consumption and x_{it+j} denotes the consumption of an individual during period *t+j* at the *i*th stage of his life. This function is strictly concave and a linear homogenous function. $v(\cdot)$ also satisfies the Inada condition. The corresponding budget constraint is

$$W_t h_t \geq p_t\left[c_{1t} + \rho c_{2t+1}\right],\ \rho \equiv \frac{p_{t+1}}{p_t}. \tag{4.10}$$

It is well known that the corresponding indirect utility function, *ID*, of $v(\cdot)$ can be represented as

$$ID \equiv \frac{W_t h_t}{\psi\left(p_t, p_{t+1}\right)}, \tag{4.11}$$

where $\psi\left(\cdot\right)$ is a monotonously increasing linear homogenous function. The optimal decision requires the following condition:

$$\frac{d}{dh_t} ID_t = G'(h_t) \Leftrightarrow \frac{W_t}{\psi\left(p_t, p_{t+1}\right)} = G'\left(h_t\right) \\ \Leftrightarrow W_t = \psi\left(p_t, p_{t+1}\right) \cdot G'\left(h_t\right). \tag{4.12}$$

Accordingly, the firm's zero-profit condition requires

$$p_t\gamma - W_t = 0 \Leftrightarrow p_t\gamma - W_t = p_t\gamma - \psi\left(p_t, p_{t+1}\right) \cdot G'\left(h_t\right) = 0 \\ \Leftrightarrow \gamma = \psi\left(1, \rho\right) \cdot G'\left(h_t\right). \tag{4.13}$$

where ρ is the *ex-ante* inflation rate as previously defined in equation (4.1).

Equation (4.13) is the implicit aggregate supply function of this model (i.e., the dynamic extension of the second postulate of the classical school). The right-hand side of the equation is an increasing function of h_t and ρ. Hence, the aggregate supply function is a downward sloping curve *AS* in figure 4.3. It should be noted that the vertical axis is the inflation rate ρ, and not the price level p_t. When inflation advances, the nominal wage, W_t, increases because future goods become expensive relative to current goods. This dampens labor demand because the real wage in terms of current goods must be equal to the marginal productivity of labor. Accordingly, the aggregate supply, y_t^S, decreases as inflation advances. This is how curve *AS* is derived.

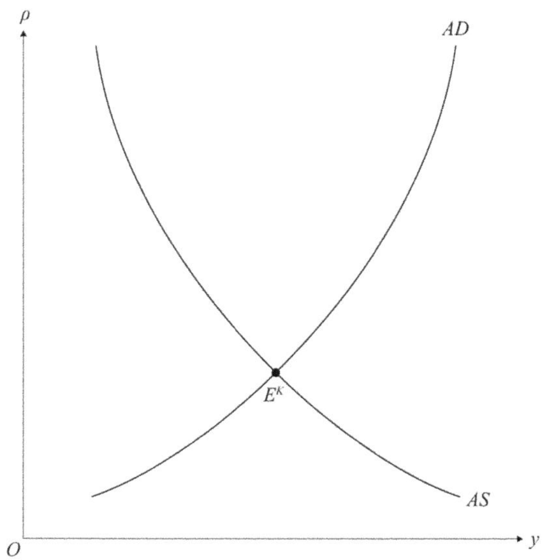

Figure 4.3 Dynamic equilibrium. *Source*: Author.

Labor productivity γ is a vital parameter of the aggregate supply function as shown in equation (4.13). Suppose that the inflation rate, ρ, is kept constant and that the labor productivity slows downs (γ becomes a smaller value than before). The decreased labor productivity curtails the hours worked, h_t, because the real wage in terms of current goods is invariant by assumption. Thus, whenever the labor productivity stagnates, curve *AS* shifts leftward.

Let us now consider the aggregate demand, y_t^D. The aggregate demand is composed of three items: the young generation's consumption; the old generation's consumption; and government consumption. The young generation's consumption, c_{1t}, becomes

$$c_{1t} = c(\rho) y_t, 1 > c' > 0, \tag{4.14}$$

because the lifetime utility function on consumption is linear homogenous. Since the older generation is assumed to have no incentive to pass on inheritance, they exchange all their money, which they carried over from the previous period, and thus,

$$c_{2t-1} = \frac{M_{t-1}}{p_t} \tag{4.15}$$

holds. The budget constraint of the government is as follows:

$$g_t \equiv \frac{M_t}{p_t} - \frac{M_{t-1}}{p_t}. \tag{4.16}$$

This identity implies that the government finances its consumption by seigniorage.

From equations (4.14), (4.15), and (4.16), the aggregate demand, y_t^D, can be defined as

$$y_t^D \equiv c(\rho) y_t + \frac{M_{t-1}}{p_t} + g_t = c(\rho) y_t + m,$$
$$\text{where } m \equiv \frac{M_t}{p_t} = \frac{M_{t+j}}{p_{t+j}}, \forall j \geq 0. \tag{4.17}$$

To find the equilibrium with the zero-profit condition of the firm, we can set

$$y_t^D = y_t^S = y_t. \tag{4.18}$$

Using equation (4.18), equation (4.17) can be transformed into

$$y_t = c(\rho) y_t + m \Leftrightarrow y_t = \frac{m}{1 - c(\rho)}. \tag{4.19}$$

Equation (4.19) is the equation of the aggregate demand. When the inflation rate increases, the equilibrium GDP, y_t, increases. Thus, the aggregate demand function *AD* becomes upward sloping. In addition, when real cash balance, *m*, increases, *ceteris paribus*, curve *AD* in figure 4.3 shifts right because of the multiplier effect. Equilibrium of the economy is achieved at point E^K, which is the intersection of curves *AS* and *AD*.

4.3 COMPARATIVE STATICS

This section considers how exogenous economic shocks affect the macroeconomic equilibrium. Three shocks are analyzed: labor productivity slowdown; radical QE policy; and stagflation provoked by the lack of belief in the intrinsic value of money.

4.3.1 Labor Productivity Slowdown

An autonomous labor productivity slowdown is represented by the reduction of parameter γ. As described in section 4.2, this causes a downward shift of

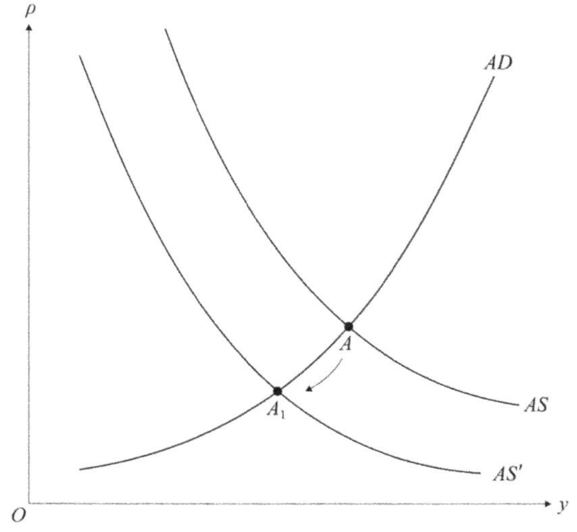

Figure 4.4 Productivity slowdown and disinflation. *Source*: Author.

the *AS* curve. Figure 4.4 illustrates the consequence. The equilibrium moves from point *A* to A_1. Accordingly, the slowdown of labor productivity and disinflation coexist in our theory.

The causality is as follows. An autonomous labor productivity slowdown decreases the aggregate supply, and excess demand emerges in the goods market. Assume that individuals are *confident* of the current intrinsic value of money, $1/p_t$, then by definition, the current price level, p_t, is unchanged[4]. It is plausible to assume that individuals anticipate the future price, p_{t+1}, to be lower because the economy will sufficiently adapt to the labor productivity slowdown. Thus, rational *ex-ante* deflationary expectations are generated, and disinflation is realized. Such disinflation reduces the aggregate consumption of the young generation, and hence equilibrates the goods market. It also should be noted that the economy falls into recession because of the decrease in aggregate consumption.

4.3.2 Effect of Radical QE Policy

The radical QE policy shifts the aggregate demand curve *AD* toward the right as in figure 4.5. The economy moves from point *B* to B_1. Business upturns in conjunction with disinflation.

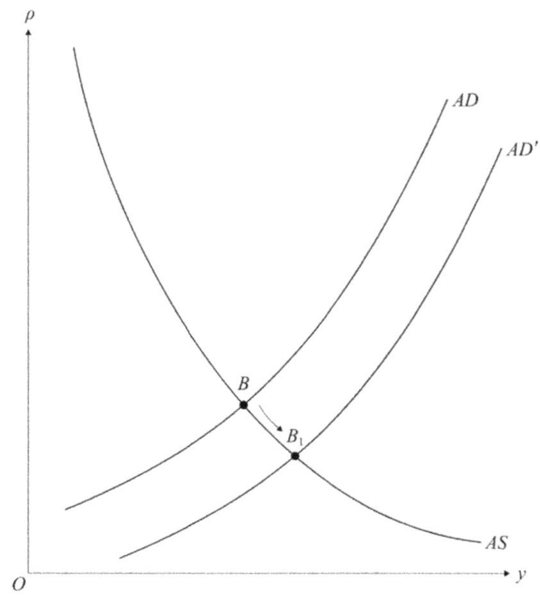

Figure 4.5 Radical QE policy and the macroeconomy. *Source*: Author.

This property of the model is quite similar to the current situation faced by the Japanese economy. The QE policy, which injects a huge amount of money into the economy, requires the same amount of new demand for money. As equation (4.19) shows, aggregate saving is an increasing function of GDP and a decreasing function of the inflation rate. Accordingly, GDP increases (the multiplier effect) and the inflation rate is reduced. Since the aggregate supply function, equation (4.13), is a decreasing function of the inflation rate, an increase in GDP and a deceleration of inflation is consistent with the change on the demand side.

In other words, the inflation rate must fall to create new demand for money to equilibrate the money market. Disinflation also helps to increase aggregate income because disinflation lowers real wage per capita in terms of current goods. It should be noted that disinflation is a phenomenon which increases the rate of return for money. Money has two aspects: a measure for exchange and its intrinsic value that it holds within. These social roles of money are inseparable.[5] When the rate of return increases, much money is carried over for future consumption.

Followers of the quantity theory of money forget this fact. Monetarism, including the new Keynesian's real cash balance in the utility function, has no microeconomic foundation for money demand. Many central banks follow the quantity theory. They believe their economy can escape disinflation if sufficient money is injected despite the fact that a radical QE policy actually provokes disinflation and/or deflation.

As long as the intrinsic value of money is in a state of *confidence*, disinflation prevails despite the intent of the central bank. However, there is no denying that there is indeed a limit of the nominal money supply where individuals can maintain confidence in money. Once the volume of the nominal money supply exceeds this critical point, hyperinflation (bursting of the money bubble) is inevitably provoked. Details will be discussed in the next subsection.

4.3.3 Stagflation: Bursting of the Money Bubble

Bruno and Sachs (1985) regard stagflation as the upward shift of the aggregate supply curve *SS* in figure 4.2 caused by circumstances such as a crude oil price hike. My model predicts such supply shocks, which aggravate labor productivity and cause disinflation. Which of the two phenomena is actually realized can only be determined by a precise and careful empirical analysis. While stagflation, which Bruno-Sachs originally illustrated, was a temporary phenomenon, most stagflations observed in Greece, South American countries, and African countries are actually persistent. Such a phenomenon comes from the lack of belief in the intrinsic value of money.

It should be noted that money belongs to a class of "bubbly" assets in the sense that fiat money is an asset that possesses no economic value in itself. However, individuals believe its intrinsic value to the extent that the circulated money is scarce relative to

i. the potential production capacity of an economy, and
ii. the levying ability of the government.

Whenever the production level approaches full capacity, the economy has no room for providing goods for additionally issued money. If either of these two conditions is not satisfied, individuals lose faith in the intrinsic value of money, which is based on the social benefits derived from overcoming *the difficulty of the double coincident of wants*. Even money loses its *confidence*, if conditions (i) or (ii) is not satisfied. That is, individuals become skeptical whether money can be used to exchange for goods at any given time.

In such a case, stagflation is provoked in the following way. Individuals rush to the goods market, and the price hikes rapidly. The real cash balance $m \equiv M_t/p_t$ decreases. This shifts curve *AD* upwards, and hence, equilibrium moves from point *C* to C_1 as in figure 4.6.

This implies that the increase in the current price level p_t deprives the purchasing power of the older generation and government, and thus results in the fall of GDP, y_t. *Ex-post* stagflation is provoked in the sense of equation (4.1). Distinct from the Bruno-Sachs model, such stagflation, which is triggered by

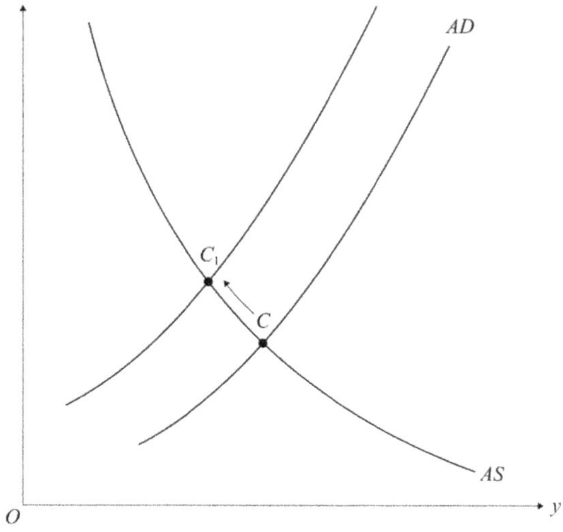

Figure 4.6 Stagflation by disbelief in the value of money. *Source*: Author.

a lack of the intrinsic value of money is persistent. To offset the reduction of the aggregate demand, the equilibrium inflation rate stays at a high level because a higher inflation rate stimulates consumption by the young generation. In other words, the young generation also loses faith in the value of money. I have implicitly assumed the policy variable to be real cash balance. Accordingly, even though the government increases the nominal money supply proportional to the inflation rate, the economy continues to be stuck in a devastating economic situation.

As discussed in subsection 4.3.2, the radical QE policy is effective to the extent that individuals are confident of the intrinsic value of money (although the effect on inflation rate does not satisfy central banks). However, there is a limit to this kind of monetary policy. When the real cash balance exceeds the upper bound that might be prescribed in conditions (i) and (ii), belief in the intrinsic value of money is impaired, and hyperinflation and persistent stagflation will ensue. It is an ironic historical fact that the socialist leader Lenin advocated this as the fastest way to annihilate the monetary system and collapse capitalism.

4.4 CONCLUDING REMARKS

This chapter examined how labor productivity slowdown affects the inflation rate. In addition, I analyzed the relationship between radical QE policy and the inflation rate. Findings are as follows.

First, the standard neoclassical model fails to explain the coexistence of labor productivity slowdown and disinflation. Intuitively, as the Bruno-Sachs (1985) model suggests, such a slowdown triggers an upward shift of the aggregate supply curve. Hence, to the extent that the aggregate demand curve stays intact, the economy falls into stagnation with an increased equilibrium price (i.e., *static* stagflation, which implies the occurrence of a one-time jump of current prices).

Second, in contrast to the neoclassical model, the Keynesian OLG model predicts that a labor productivity slowdown triggers disinflation. The causality is as follows. A labor productivity slowdown curtails aggregate supply. Whenever individuals are confident of the intrinsic value of money, by definition, the current price remains at the same level, and thus excess demand emerges. Individuals rationally anticipate that the economy will adapt to the productivity slowdown, reduce the potential excess demand, and hence expect the *equilibrium* future price level to be lowered relative to the current level. As such, disinflation occurs. Since the consumption demand of the young generation is an increasing function of the inflation rate, disinflation curtails the current aggregate demand. Through this process, the equilibrium of the overall economy is achieved. Namely, I ascertain the causality by which the slowdown in labor productivity is connected with disinflation.

Third, I have ascertained that the radical QE policy advances disinflation. The radical QE policy has two aspects. One aspect is that real cash balance is drastically increased as long as *confidence* in money is retained. The rate of return for money (the inverse of the inflation rate) increases to equilibrate the money market (the reverse side of the goods market), and thus disinflation advances. The other aspect is that the increased real cash balance expands the aggregate demand and recovers the business through the multiplier process. Accordingly, business booms and disinflation coexist under the radical QE policy, as long as individuals retain *confidence.*

Finally, I clarified how persistent stagflation is provoked by a lack of belief in the intrinsic value of money. As discussed above, the Bruno-Sachs (1985) model describes stagflation as a transition process caused by a supply shock such as crude oil price hike. A negative supply shock shifts the aggregate supply curve leftward. As a result, the price of goods also hikes and the equilibrium GDP decreases. Nevertheless, their model is basically static, and the hike of the output price is temporary. Actual stagflation provokes more persistent inflation along with mass unemployment. In fact, most developing economies are burdened by this kind of structural stagflation. Lack of belief in the intrinsic value of money is considered to be provoked by the following two conditions:

(1) a huge amount of money stock relative to an economy's potential production capacity, and
(2) an inadequate levying ability of the government.

If condition (1) and/or (2) is satisfied, individuals become skeptical about the exchangeability of money for goods. Consumers are confident of the intrinsic value of money, which stems from the convenience factor as a means for exchange, and/or its value hoarding nature. When condition (1) and/or (2) threatens the repayment ability of the government, individuals regard such a situation as the bankruptcy of the government. Individuals rush to the goods market and the price level hikes. This reduces the purchasing power of the older generation and the government whose income is fixed in the nominal term, and aggregate demand decreases. Potential excess supply emerges. Thus, the economy falls into serious stagnation. In addition, the young generation rationally expects that the economy would adapt to such a devastating situation, and that the *equilibrium* future price level would continue to be high, clearing the potential excess supply. Thus, lack of belief in the intrinsic value of money provokes stagflation.

To summarize, there is a critical limit in the QE monetary policy. The critical point is determined by whether conditions (1) and/or (2) are satisfied. It should be noted that hyperinflation is a kind of stagflation in the sense that economic stagnation and rapid price increase coexist. As discussed above, lack of belief in the intrinsic value of money is persistent once it is generated. This is the reason prudent management is the most important virtue for traditional and conservative financial institutions. This still seems to be conventional wisdom for current financial institutions.

NOTES

1. For example, Byrne, Fernald, and Reinsdorf (2016) argue it is difficult to find productivity slowdown in the US despite substantial measurement errors.
2. Gali (2008) is a standard text of new Keynesian economics. The real cash balance is introduced in the utility function. This implies that the quantity theory of money is upheld in new Keynesian economics in the long run because the maximization behavior concerning the real cash balance allows the real cash balance to be completely expressed by constant deep parameters.
3. If the aggregate production is concave, it is easy to show that the aggregate supply curve *SS* becomes upward sloping. However, parameter γ becomes the TFP at this time.
4. My model can determine only the relative value of money (the inverse of the inflation rate). It is necessary to determine the value of the sequence of price levels to establish the initial condition of the price level. This value is arbitrarily given. The condition for "*confidence*" is developed by Otaki (2015a), which implies that the current absolute value of money, $1/p_t$, is independent of the nominal money supply.
5. For proof of the inseparability of money's two roles, see Otaki (2015a, ch. 15).

Chapter 5

An Equilibrium Selection Procedure Based on Ramsey's Probability Theory

ABSTRACT

The basic model in chapter 2 supports not only Keynesian equilibrium but also the quantity theoretical one. Based on Ramsey's probability theory, which describes the degree of human confidence, I determine which of the two types of equilibrium is more plausible. In other words, the equilibrium selection problem is solved by a method of *partial language* that means a language that does not assume perfect confidence in the considered causality relationship.

5.1 INTRODUCTION

No economic agent behaves with perfect confidence on the consequences of its economic activity. How does such an agent make the decision in reality? In our context, it is vital to what extent Keynesian belief that money preserves its purchasing power despite an increase in the nominal supply is plausible. This is important because, as shown in chapter 2, an alternative rational expectations equilibrium can exist: the quantity theory of money. That is, both types of equilibrium are self-fulfilling, and thus both expectations possibly become truth depending on people's beliefs. Based on Otaki (2015b), I analyze this type of equilibrium selection procedure.

The issue is which of the two beliefs do people tend to commit to? The key aspect concerns the conciseness of such beliefs. If one finds more complexity in comprehension on the way of thought of one type of rational belief, it becomes less persuasive and more vulnerable. In this respect, the plausibility of a rational belief, which determines the law of motion of the actual economy, is decisively based on its conciseness.

Ramsey's (1928) probability theory is suitable for measuring the degree of confidence in a given belief that is revealed through actions. For example, assume that proposition *A* is true but that people are uncertain about the truth. Two possible economic behaviors might arise. One option is that people behave in line with proposition *A* with frequency *p* and thus achieve a good result while they misconduct with frequency $1-p$, resulting in poor performance. The other option is that people ascertain that proposition *A* is true at cost $f(d)$ in each trial, and consequently achieve a good performance.

Ramsey assumes that people's intuition improves (i.e., *p* is heightened) through experience to the degree that the return from each behavior is the same. Accordingly, the cost for knowing the truth, $f(d)$, is crucial for determining the degree of confidence because the difficulty in achieving the truth determines the upper limit of the insight's correctness. As such, more complicated self-filling expectations hardly realize because people become less confident in such a line of thought. By using this procedure, I examine the plausibility of the Keynesian equilibrium compared with that of the quantity theoretical equilibrium.

This chapter is organized as follows. Section 5.2 introduces Ramsey's probability theory. Section 5.3 constructs a model in which both Keynesian and monetarism equilibria are supported. Meanwhile, I show that the former equilibrium is more plausible and prevalent than the latter. Section 5.4 includes brief concluding remarks.

5.2 RAMSEY'S THEORY

Frequency theory is at the basis of both the familiar probability theory established by Kolmogrov relying on the measure theory and Ramsey's (1928) theory. The measure theoretical approach is ultimately meaningless without the law of large numbers (i.e., an ergodic property) because the exact shapes of the density and/or cumulative distribution function is unknowable.

Because samples are usually small, Ramsey completely discards the law of large numbers by replacing it with his theory by relying only on the *ex-post* (realized) average of finite trials. This property of Ramsey's theory is quite suitable for the social sciences because the number of available samples is limited and the environment surrounding the trials is almost uncontrollable.

Let us denote the frequency of correct conducts by p, which is defined as the ratio of the number of the correct conducts, m, to the total number of incidences, n.

$$p \equiv \frac{m}{n}. \tag{5.1}$$

The most prominent feature of Ramseys' theory is the connection of this probability (frequency) with one's *action* toward the true proposition in question. Specifically, Ramsey assumes that one can ascertain whether the proposition is right after paying some investigation cost, $f(d)$, where d denotes the difficulty of knowing the true causality. In addition, he also assumes that whenever one acts in accordance with the belief that the proposition is true, the gain from such behavior must be equal to the gain obtained by knowing the truth. Unless such a relationship holds, the subject surely stops behaving according to the belief, and instead, ascertains true causality at the cost $f(d)$ when deciding on the action to take. Thus, it is natural to assume that f is an increasing function of d.

Let the benefits obtained from a behavior in line with the true proposition be denoted as a and b in case of misconduct ($a > b$). The gain from the n trials, π, is

$$\pi = npa + n\left[1 - p\right]b. \tag{5.2}$$

If, instead, the subject accesses the true causality in each trial, the gain, π^T, becomes

$$\pi^T = na - nf\left(d\right). \tag{5.3}$$

By equalizing equation (5.2) and (5.3) and taking equation (5.1) into consideration, the limit probability (i.e., the belief about the validity of the proposition), p, becomes

$$p = 1 - \frac{f\left(d\right)}{a - b}. \tag{5.4}$$

Equation (5.4) embodies an important concept: along with an increase in the difficulty in understanding and checking the proposition in question, individuals become less confident in it. This is because the more complex the proposition, the more costly the examining of its truthfulness when individuals wish so. Such a tendency is quite prevalent in everyday life.

5.3 PLAUSIBILITY OF KEYNESIAN ECONOMICS

In relation to economic theory, there is an acute difference in the difficulty of understanding Keynesian theory and monetarism. As Otaki (2007, 2015) shows, the Keynesian theory upholds when people merely believe that the value of money, which is defined by the inverse of the price index, is not affected by a change in the nominal money supply. In other words, as long as people rationally believe in its intrinsic value, money becomes non-neutral.

In contrast to such a simple structure, as chapter 2 shows, monetarism requires much information and complex processing to be understood and believed in. Specifically, every individual is incessantly concerned about the nominal money supply changes and all must investigate whether the price level proportionately moves. Moreover, they all must know the exact value of the Marshallian k. To summarize, the value, d, can be deemed to be much larger under monetarism than under the Keynesian thesis.

This implies that, *ceteris paribus*, laypeople are more confident in Keynesian economics than in monetarism. As such, if people behave according to their confidence in a theory, the actual economy tends to exhibit the properties of a Keynesian economy.

5.3.1 Two Alternative Equilibria

A two-period overlapping-generations model with an infinite time horizon is considered. The model is based on Otaki (2007, 2015a) There is no population growth and every individual has an identical utility function:

$$U_t \equiv [c_{1t}]^{\alpha} [c_{2t}]^{1-\alpha} - \delta_t \cdot \beta, 0 < \alpha < 1, c_{it} \equiv \left[\int_0^1 [c_{it}(\omega)]^{1-\eta^{-1}} d\omega \right]^{\frac{1}{1-\eta^{-1}}}, \quad (5.5)$$

where $c_{it}(\omega)$ is the consumption level of goods ω by an individual born at the beginning of period t, during his ith stage of life. δ_t is a definition function the value of which takes unity when the individual is employed and zero when unemployed. β is the disutility of labor supply.

For simplicity, it is assumed that the marginal productivity of labor is unity and that there is no fixed cost. Each good is produced by firm ω monopolistically. In addition, this model assumes that the labor market is at an interior equilibrium with some individuals being always unemployed, and that the equilibrium nominal wage should be located above the nominal reservation wage.

These assumptions yield the following equation:

$$p_t(\omega) = \frac{W_t}{1-\eta^{-1}}, \tag{5.6}$$

where $p_t(\omega)$ is the price of good ω and W_t is the nominal wage during period t. From the property of the indirect utility function, which corresponds to equation (5.5), the nominal reservation wage, W_t^R, becomes

$$W_t^R = \beta\gamma P_t^{\alpha} P_{t+1}^{1-\alpha}, P_t \equiv \left[\int_0^1 \left[p_t(\omega)\right]^{1-\eta} d\omega\right]^{\frac{1}{1-\eta}}, \gamma \equiv \alpha^{\alpha}\left[1-\alpha\right]^{1-\alpha}. \tag{5.7}$$

Combining equations (5.6) and (5.7), the equilibrium inflation rate, π^*, should be located within

$$\pi^* \equiv \frac{P_{t+1}^*}{P_t^*} \leq \left[\frac{1-\eta^{-1}}{\beta\gamma}\right]^{\frac{1}{1-\alpha}}. \tag{5.8}$$

Furthermore, an elementary calculus gives us the following aggregate consumption function of the young generation, C_t:

$$C_t \equiv \alpha \cdot \frac{W_t^R}{P_t} L_t = \alpha \cdot y_t, \tag{5.9}$$

where y_t is the real GDP in terms of current goods. Consequently, the goods market equilibrium condition can be obtained:

$$y_t = \alpha \cdot y_t + \frac{M_t}{P_t}, \tag{5.10}$$

where M_t is the nominal money supply at the beginning of period t. The second term on the right-hand side of equation (5.10) is the real total expenditure of the older generation, $(M_{t-1})/P_t$, with government expenditure financed by printing money being $(M_t - M_{t-1})/P_t$. It is assumed that the economy is in its stationary state after period t, and thus that the monetary authority keeps the real money supply constant. In other words, the growth rate is fixed at the same level as π^* both in Keynesian equilibrium and the monetarism.

Equation (5.10) contains two undetermined endogenous variables, that is, the real GDP y_t and the initial price level P_t. This means that the structure of an economy basically depends on how individuals evaluate money. If they believe that the intrinsic value is independent of the nominal money supply, the initial price level remains intact even after a change in the nominal money supply in rational expectations equilibrium, and money becomes non-neutral (i.e., the Keynesian proposition).

On the other hand, when people believe that the value of money is not absolute but relative, the following equilibrium price function (i.e., the monetarism proposition) holds:

$$P_t = \kappa^{-1} \cdot M_t. \tag{5.11}$$

We must note both equilibria are self-fulfilling. From equations (5.10) and (5.11), it is clear that the equilibrium GDP under the Keynesian proposition, y^k, is larger than that under monetarism, y^m, as long as the initial price level is sufficiently low and the value of money sufficiently high. Henceforth, it is possible to assume that $y^k > y^m$. In addition, the corresponding Marshallian *k*s are denoted as κ^k and κ^m, respectively ($\kappa^k > \kappa^m$).[1]

5.3.2. Ramsey's Belief and Keynesian Economics

This subsection applies Ramsey's formula (5.4) to examine the plausibility of the two macroeconomic theses. Before undertaking the analysis, it is necessary to clarify what kind of knowledge is needed for a layperson in economics to understand each theory.

i. For the Keynesian theory, the layperson must be able to recognize that the current price level is unchanged despite a change in the nominal money supply.
ii. For monetarism, the layperson must (a) be able to confirm that the current price level changes proportionately with the nominal money supply, (b) be comfortable with the concept of linear function to understand the relationship in (a), and (c) know the value of the proportional constant κ (Marshallian *k*) as well as the exact quantity of the nominal money supply.

As such, it is evident that the monetarist thesis is far more difficult to understand than the Keynesian one. Accordingly, the value of *d* in equation (5.4) is thought to be much larger in the case of monetarism.

In addition, whenever the true proposition is the Keynesian thesis, which implies that other individuals believe in the intrinsic value of money, the parameters *a* and *b* in equation (5.2) are proportional to y^k and y^m, respectively.

Therefore, as per equation (5.4), without loss of generality, the degree of confidence in the Keynesian equilibrium, p^m, becomes

$$p^k = 1 - \frac{f(d^k)}{y^k - y^m}, \tag{5.12}$$

where d^k reflects the difficulty in understanding the Keynesian thesis that is easier to absorb than the quantity theory of money, which is embodied in the value of d^m.[2]

Conversely, when the quantity theory is the correct proposition (i.e., other people forecast the use of equation [5.11]), the parameters a and b take the following values:

$$a = y^m,\ b = y^m - \left[y^k - y^m\right] \Rightarrow a - b = y^k - y^m. \tag{5.13}$$

The value of b is due to the excess production when people misperceive the monetarism economy as the more expansionary Keynesian economy. Accordingly, the degree of confidence in the quantity theory of money, p^m, becomes

$$p^m = 1 - \frac{f(d^m)}{y^k - y^m}. \tag{5.14}$$

Consequently, $f(d^k) \ll f(d^m)$, and thus, $p^m \ll p^k$. To summarize, the Keynesian equilibrium is more plausible or self-enforceable than the one derived through the quantity theory of money as individuals rarely misconduct once such a view prevails. This is because the Keynesian view on the value of money is much more comprehensible for laypeople in economics.

5.4 CONCLUDING REMARKS

This chapter develops the concept of plausibility in alternative monetary theories with Ramsey's (1928) belief as the basis for analysis. This theory assumes that the depth of belief (i.e., the degree of confidence) can be measured by human's action toward the true proposition, which in turn depends on the cost incurred to know the truth. When such a cost is not high, people are more confident about the true proposition because they can achieve the truth more easily if they wish.

While Keynesian economics is upheld only by the belief in the stability of the value of money in terms of goods, monetarism is not sustained until laypeople in economics understand not only the exact linear relationship between nominal money supply and price index but also macroeconomic statistics, which they are mostly unconcerned with in everyday life. Consequently, the cost for knowing the truth is much lower in the Keynesian setting. Thus, Keynesian economics is more plausible than monetarism although both theories are characterized by the self-fulfilling property. In this sense, Ramsey's theory can be considered an effective equilibrium selection procedure.

NOTES

1. Note that knowing the resulting benefits in empirical terms does not necessarily mean that all individuals are informed about the whole structure of the economy.
2. Note that, as shown in chapter 3, when the equilibrium concept of goods markets is monopolistic competition, there emerges an economic surplus that is proportional to the real GDP.

Appendix A

The Weak Law of Large Numbers

Consider an identically and independently distributed stochastic process whose variance is finite. Let us denote the real number of the *j*th trial as X_j. In addition, its arithmetic average by the *n*-th trial is defined as S_n. Namely,

$$S_n \equiv \frac{X_1 + X_2 + \cdots + X_j + \cdots X_n}{n} \equiv \frac{\sum_{j=1}^{n} X_j}{n}. \tag{A.1}$$

When we denote the cumulative distribution function of X_j as $F(X_j)$, the mathematical expectation μ and the variance σ^2 are expressed by

$$E[X] \equiv \int X_j dF(X_j),\ \sigma^2 \equiv \int [X_j - \mu]^2 dF(X_j).$$

The weak law of large numbers asserts that as the number of the trials increases, the probability of the distance between S_n and μ converges to zero. The proof is as follows.

$$E\left[\left|\frac{S_n}{n} - \mu\right|^2\right] = \frac{\sigma^2}{n} \geq \int_{\left|\frac{S_n}{n}-\mu\right|>\varepsilon} \int \cdots \int \left|\frac{S_n}{n} - \mu\right| dF(X_1) dF(X_2) \cdots dF(X_n)$$

$$\geq \varepsilon^2 \int_{\left|\frac{S_n}{n}-\mu\right|>\varepsilon} dF(X_1) dF(X_2) \cdots dF(X_n) \Leftrightarrow \frac{\sigma^2}{n\varepsilon^2} \geq \Pr\left(\left|\frac{S_n}{n} - \mu\right| > \varepsilon\right).$$

Since, for any fixed ε, the left-hand side of the inequality converges to zero when $n \to \infty$, we obtain

$$\lim_{n \to \infty} \Pr\left(\left| \frac{S_n}{n} - \mu \right| > \varepsilon \right) = 0.$$

This completes the proof.

Appendix B

Gist of the New Keynesian Theory

In this appendix, I introduce a deterministic new Keynesian model. Since the aim is to understand crucial qualitative properties of the theory, the model is simplified. Nevertheless, an extension to a general case is not so difficult. The most prominent assumption of this school is that there are significant lags to realign prices. In addition, the school regards the real cash balance, which is defined by the ratio of nominal money hoarding to a price index, as an argument of the utility function. In other words, individuals gain utility from hoarding money as an act on its own.

Let us move to model building. Assume there are two firms that produce differentiated goods in an economy: firm 1 and 2. The linearly approximated demand function is

$$x_{it} = -\frac{p_{it}}{P_t} + \frac{M}{P_i}, P_t \equiv \frac{p_{it} + p_{jt}}{2}. \tag{B.1}$$

Equation (B.1) represents the demand for company i's goods during the t-th period, x_{it}, is a decreasing function of the relative price between an offer price p_{it} and a general price index P_t, and an increasing function of the real cash balance, M/P_t, because the school assumes that consumption is stimulated in conjunction with the satisfaction of money hoarding.

Furthermore, to facilitate the calculation, I assume that firms maximize their sales although this assumption is not essential. Then the sales are

$$p_{it}x_{it} = p_{it}\left[-\frac{p_{it}}{P_t} + \frac{M}{P_i}\right]. \tag{B.2}$$

Accordingly, when a firm neglects the effect of its price revision on the general price index, optimal pricing leads us to the following equation:

$$p_{it}^{*} = \frac{M}{2}. \tag{B.3}$$

We can easily ascertain that equation (B.3) holds for both firm and the equilibrium output is the same level as unity when the economy is in a stationary state. Assume that the economy in the stationary state is perturbed by an increase in nominal money supply from M to $\bar{M}$. If only firm 1 can update the offer price, firm 1 adopts the optimal pricing in equation (B.3), and thus,

$$p_{1t}^{*} = \frac{\bar{M}}{2}, \tag{B.4}$$

holds. By contrast, firm 2 cannot revise its offer price by assumption, and thus, the total output (real GDP) is obtained by substituting equations (B.3) and (B.4) into equation (B.1) as follows:

$$x_{1t}^{*} = \frac{\frac{\bar{M}}{2}}{\frac{1}{2}\left[\frac{\bar{M}}{2} + \frac{M}{2}\right]} > 1, \quad x_{2t}^{*} = \frac{\bar{M} - \frac{M}{2}}{\frac{1}{2}\left[\frac{\bar{M}}{2} + \frac{M}{2}\right]} > 1 \Rightarrow x_{1t}^{*} + x_{2t}^{*} > 2. \tag{B.5}$$

This result is derived from the fact that the inability of firm 2 to update its price raises the real cash balance. The increased real cash balance heightens consumption due to the complement property between demand for hoarding money and consumption. Consequently, an expansionary monetary policy can generate positive effects to the total output in the short run.

However, soon after the next period arrives, this positive effect disappears. In period t+1, firm 2 realigns its offer price in accordance with equation (B.4). Thus, the general price index, $P_{t+1} \equiv (1/2)\,[p_{1t+1} + p_{2t+1}]$, rises. Actually, we obtain

$$x_{1t}^{*} = \frac{\frac{\bar{M}}{2}}{\frac{1}{2}\left[\frac{\bar{M}}{2} + \frac{\bar{M}}{2}\right]} = 1, x_{2t}^{*} = \frac{\frac{\bar{M}}{2}}{\frac{1}{2}\left[\frac{\bar{M}}{2} + \frac{\bar{M}}{2}\right]} = 1 \Rightarrow x_{1t}^{*} + x_{2t}^{*} = 2. \tag{B.6}$$

Equation (B.6) shows that an increase in money supply is eventually absorbed by a proportional rise in price. That is, the economy regresses to the former stationary state, and money becomes neutral. The effectiveness of monetary policy acutely depends on lags of price adjustment, which is provided exogenously. It should be noted that, differing from new Keynesian assertions, inflation is not a cause of a boom but a result, and hence, provoking inflation requires caution.

Finally, if price adjustment is synchronized, both firms can revise their offer prices in accordance with equation (B.3). In such a case, money is always neutral. Therefore, the new Keynesian model diverges from the quantity theory of money only on the point of *a priori* price rigidity. In this sense, new Keynesian is akin to old Keynesian which assumes stickiness in nominal wages.

Appendix C

Derivation of Equations (3.4) and (3.5)

Figure C.1 illustrates the meaning of equation (3.4). We can restrict the domain of random variable, x, to positive orthant without losing generality. It is apparent from the figure that the Stieltjes integral that implies the mathematical expectation of x

$$\int_{\underline{x}}^{\bar{x}} x dF(x) \equiv \lim_{n\to\infty} \sum_{i=1}^{n} x_i \left[F(x_{i+1}) - F(x_i) \right], \quad \underline{x} < x_1 < \cdots < x_n < \bar{x}, \tag{C.1}$$

corresponds to the square below the inverse function of CDF. Therefore, we have

$$\int_{\underline{x}}^{\bar{x}} F(x) dx = \bar{x} - \int_{\underline{x}}^{\bar{x}} x dF(x). \tag{C.2}$$

(note that $\bar{x}$ is the square of the rectangle).

Next, let us consider equation (3.5). Because equation (3.3) is held on θ_1 and θ_2, it is evident from (C.2) that

$$\int_{\underline{x}}^{0} F_{\theta_1}(x) dx = \bar{x} - \int_{\underline{x}}^{0} x dF_{\theta_1}(x) > \bar{x} - \int_{\underline{x}}^{0} x dF_{\theta_2}(x)$$

$$\text{Þ} \int_{\underline{x}}^{0} x dF_{\theta_1}(x) < \int_{\underline{x}}^{0} x dF_{\theta_2}(x) \tag{C.3}$$

$$\hat{U} \int_{0}^{\bar{x}} x dF_{\theta_2}(x) < \int_{0}^{\bar{x}} x dF_{\theta_1}(x).$$

This completes the proof. Equation (3.5) is upheld for an arbitrary convex function and is an application of Jensen's inequality. The generalization is left for readers.

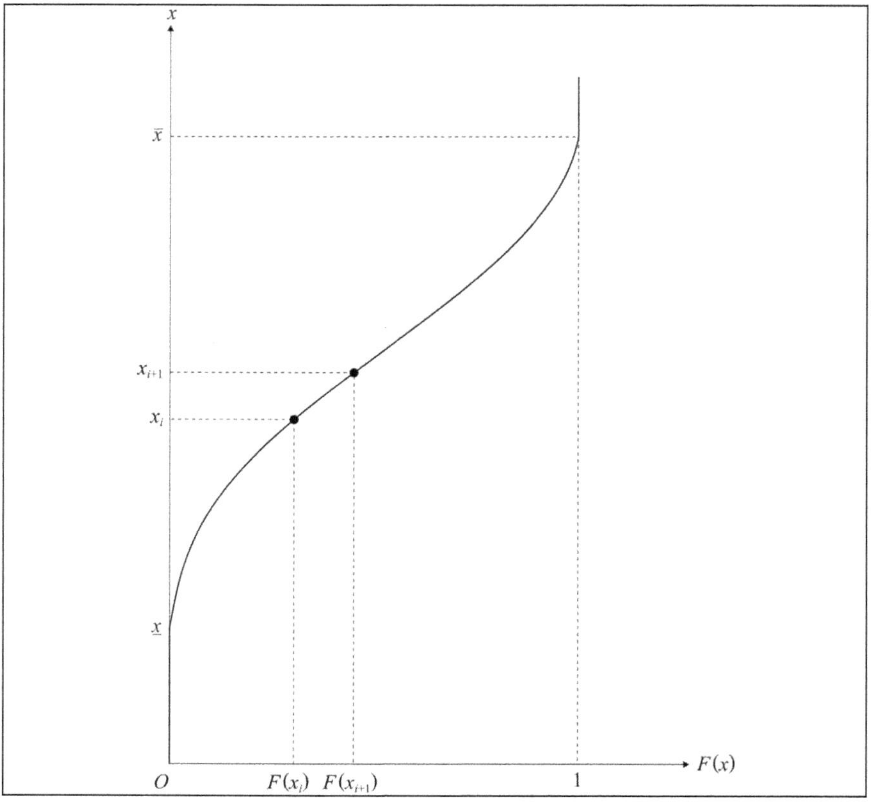

Figure C.1 Inverse Cumulative Distribution Function

References

Akerlof, George A., "The Market for 'Lemons': Qualitative Uncertainty and the Market Mechanism," *Quarterly Journal of Economics* 94, no. 3 (August 1970): 488–500.

Allen, Frederick, L., *Only Yesterday: An Informal History of the Nineteen Twenties*, New York: Harper & Brothers Publishers, 1931.

Aoki, Masahiko, "A Model of the Firm as a Stockholder-Employee Corporative Game," *American Economic Review* 70 no. 4 (September 1980): 600–610.

———. *Information, Incentives, and Bargaining in the Japanese Economy*, Cambridge: Cambridge University Press, 1988.

Barro, Robert. J., "Are Government Bonds Net Wealth?" *Journal of Political Economy* 82 no. 6 (November–December 1974): 1095–1117.

Blanchard, Oliver, J. and Nobuhiro Kiyotaki, "Monopolistic Competition and the Effect of Aggregate Demand," *American Economic Review* 77 no. 4 (September 1987): 647–66.

Blanchard, Oliver J. and Mark W. Watson, "Bubbles, Rational Expectations, and Financial Markets," NBER Working Paper No. w945 (1982).

Bruno, Michael and Jeffery D. Sachs, *Economics of Worldwide Stagflation*, Cambridge, MA: Harvard University Press, 1985.

Byrne, David M., Marshall B. Reinsdorf, and John G. Fernald, "Does the United States Have a Productivity Slowdown or a Measurement Problem?" Federal Reserve Bank of San Francisco Working Paper, 2016–03 (2016).

Calvo, Guillermo A., "Staggered Prices in a Utility-Maximizing Framework," *Journal of Monetary Economics* 12 no. 3 (September 1983): 383–98.

Christensen, Jens, "Inflation Expectations and the Risk of Deflation," *FRESF* Economic Letter, 2009–34 (2009).

Dewey, John, *Democracy and Education: An Introduction to the Philosophy of Education*, London: Macmillan, 1916, Reprinted by Free Press, New York, 1944.

Diamond, Peter, A., "Aggregate-Demand Management in Search Equilibrium," *Journal of Political Economy* 90 no. 5 (October 1982): 927–54.

ECB Economic Bulletin, "The Slowdown in US Labour Productivity Growth—Stylised Facts and Economic Implications," Issue 2 / 2016—Box 1 (2016).

Friedman, Milton and Rose D. Friedman, *Free to Choose: A Personal Statement*, San Diego: Harcourt, 1980.

Friedman, Milton, "The Role of Monetary Policy," *American Economic Review* 58 no.1 (March 1968): 1–17.

Fukao, Kyoji and Masayuki Otaki, "Accumulation of Human Capital and the Business Cycle," *Journal of Political Economy* 101 no. 1 (February 1993): 73–99.

Gali, Jordi, *Monetary Policy, Inflation, and the Business Cycle: An Introduction to the New Keynesian Framework*, Princeton: Princeton University Press, 2008.

Hori, Masahiro and Satoshi Shimizutani, "Price Expectations and Consumption Under Deflation: Evidence From Japanese Household Survey Data," *International Economics and Economic Policy* 2 no. 2–3 (2005): 127–51.

Horiuchi, Kozo and Masayuki Otaki, *Doctor Shimomura's Legacy and the Post War Japanese Economy*, Singapore: Springer, 2017.

Kahn, Richard, F., "The Relationship of Home Investment to Unemployment," *Economic Journal* 41 no. 162 (June 1931): 173–98.

Kamakura, Haruko, "The Process and Current Situation of the Public Fund Injection for Stabilizing the Financial System (Kinyu Sistemu Anteika no tameno Kouteki Shikin Chunyu no Keika to Genjo)," in *Japanese, Chosa to Joho* (March 2005), Diet Library.

Keynes, John M., *The General Theory of Employment, Interest and Money*, London: Macmillan, 1936. Reprinted by Cambridge University Press 2013.

Laursen, Svend and Lloyd A. Metzler, "Flexible Exchange Rates and the Theory of Employment," *Review of Economic Statistics* 32 no. 4 (November 1950): 281–99.

Lerner, Abba. P., *The Economics of Control: Principles of Welfare Economics*, New York, Macmillan, 1944.

Lucas, Robert E. Jr., "Expectations and the Neutrality of Money," *Journal of Economic Theory* 4 (1972): 103–24.

Moore, George E., *Principia Ethica*. Cambridge: Cambridge University Press, 1902. Reprinted by Cambridge University Press, 1993.

Otaki, Masayuki, "The Dynamically Extended Keynesian Cross and the Welfare-Improving Fiscal Policy," *Economics Letters* 96 no. 1 (July 2007): 23–29.

———. "A Microeconomic Foundation of the Full-Employment Policy." *Economics Letters* 102 no. 1 (January 2009): 1–3.

———. *Keynesian Economics and Price Theory: Re-orientation of a Theory of Monetary Economy*, Tokyo: Springer, 2015a.

———. "Ramsey's Belief and the Plausibility of Keynesian Economics," *Theoretical Economics Letters* 5 (2015b): 725–29.

———. "A Theory of Origin of Speculative Bubbles and Public Debt Accumulation," *Theoretical Economics Letters* 6 (2016a): 1169–79.

———. *Keynes's General Theory Reconsidered in the Context of the Japanese Economy*, Singapore: Springer, 2016b.

———. *Reconsidering Keynes's General Theory in the Context of the Japanese Economy*, Singapore: Springer, 2016c.

Piazza, Roberto, "Deflation Expectations and Japan's Lost Decade," Bank of Italy Occasional Paper No. 274 (June 25, 2015).

Ramsey, Frank. P., "Truth and Probability" (1926), in *Philosophical Papers*, edited by D. H. Mellor, Cambridge, Cambridge University Press, 1990.

Sims, Christopher A., "Money, Income, and Causality," *American Economic Review* 62 no. 4 (September 1972): 540–52.

Stiglitz, Joseph E. and Andrew Weiss, "Credit Rationing in Markets with Imperfect Information," *American Economic Review* 71 no. 3 (June 1981): 393–410.

Stiglitz, Joseph E., "A Re-examination of the Modigliani-Miller Theorem," *American Economic Review* 59 no. 5 (December 1969): 784–93.

Tobin, J., "A General Equilibrium Approach to Monetary Theory," *Journal of Money, Credit, and Banking* 1 no. 1 (1969): 15–29.

Uzawa, Hirofumi, "Time Preference and the Penrose Effect in a Two-Class Model of Economic Growth," *Journal of Political Economy* 77 no. 4 (July–August 1969), 628–52.

Index

About the Author

Masayuki Otaki was professor of economics at the University of Tokyo. He completed this book shortly before passing.

Themes: Macroeconomic Theory, Economic Thought, Environmental Economic Theory.

Books: *Keynesian Economics and Price Theory: Re-orientation of a Theory of Monetary Economy* (2015); *The Origin of the Prolonged Stagnation in Contemporary Japanese Economy: Factitious Deflation and the Meltdown of the Japanese Firm as an Entity* (2015).

www.ingramcontent.com/pod-product-compliance
Ingram Content Group UK Ltd.
Pitfield, Milton Keynes, MK11 3LW, UK
UKHW020256051026
15470UKWH00020B/60

9 781498 549141